MW00458855

1000 WORDS

1000 WORDS

A WRITER'S GUIDE
TO STAYING
CREATIVE, FOCUSED,
AND PRODUCTIVE
ALL YEAR ROUND

JAMI ATTENBERG

SIMON ELEMENT

NEW YORK   LONDON   TORONTO   SYDNEY   NEW DELHI

**SIMON
ELEMENT**

An Imprint of Simon & Schuster, Inc.
1230 Avenue of the Americas
New York, NY 10020

Compilation copyright © 2024 by Jami Attenberg

Copyright credits continued on pages 259–61

Portions of this work were previously published,
in slightly different form, in other media.

All rights reserved, including the right to reproduce this book
or portions thereof in any form whatsoever. For information,
address Simon Element Subsidiary Rights Department,
1230 Avenue of the Americas, New York, NY 10020.

First Simon Element hardcover edition January 2024

SIMON ELEMENT is a trademark of Simon & Schuster, Inc.

Simon & Schuster: Celebrating 100 Years of Publishing in 2024

For information about special discounts for bulk purchases,
please contact Simon & Schuster Special Sales at 1-866-506-1949
or business@simonandschuster.com.

The Simon & Schuster Speakers Bureau can bring authors
to your live event. For more information or to book an event,
contact the Simon & Schuster Speakers Bureau at 1-866-248-3049
or visit our website at www.simonspeakers.com.

Manufactured in the United States of America

10 9 8 7 6 5 4 3 2 1

Library of Congress Cataloging-in-Publication Data has been applied for.

ISBN 978-1-6680-2360-0
ISBN 978-1-6680-2362-4 (ebook)

For Sid

CONTENTS

1000 WORDS

INTRODUCTION

#1000 WORDS OF SUMMER

Have you ever made something that has changed your life forever completely by accident?

In the spring of 2018 my dear friend, the talented memoirist and educator Anne Gisleson, and I needed some inspiration. We wanted to build enough momentum for a productive summer and direct our energy toward one location—our creative projects. To shut out the noise, slough off the distractions.

Anne was trying to finish a new nonfiction proposal. She has two children and was closing in on the end of another year teaching at a local arts high school, with all the pressures and challenges that went along with it. I had my seventh book in thirteen years to complete. We were nearly at the halfway mark of the Trump presidency and had been writing through all the chaos of that time. We both needed a push to the other side.

We brainstormed for a bit. An actor friend had recently done an exercise boot camp to get in shape for a movie. Every morning in a park in Los Angeles, for fourteen days, he did an intense cardio workout in the Southern California sun. It sounded grueling, but it had been effective.

"What if we did our own boot camp?" I asked Anne. What if we wrote 1000 words a day for two weeks straight? That length of time seemed like a doable amount. A month felt like a job, and a week felt like not enough work would get done.

"I'm in," she said immediately.

We picked a date that worked for her after the school year ended.

Then I casually posted on social media that I was doing a two-week intensive writing push with an accountability partner. Within an hour, hundreds of people had chimed in that they wanted to do it, too. I decided to set up a mailing list and send out emails to encourage anyone who had signed up. Then I asked some writer friends—many of them bestselling and critically acclaimed—to share words of wisdom for the emails.

By the end of those first two weeks, two thousand people had signed up. All of us were writing with a renewed commitment to our craft. We posted our word count to social media every day and connected with each other, and in the process we became one another's accountability partners. Someone had suggested I call it "1000 Words of Summer," a play on the 2009 movie title *(500) Days of Summer*. As with everything about this project, if it sounded like a good and simple solution, I ran with it. We adopted the #1000wordsofsummer hashtag to track our work and support one another, and it grew from there.

What started as a simple challenge between two friends has grown into a literary movement—write 1000 words a day, every day, for two weeks straight, without judgment or bias and see what comes of it. This past year we had more than thirty thousand participants.

The #1000wordsofsummer project takes place in the summertime to honor my teacher friends. While I didn't choose the path of being an educator, many of my peers did. They're out there working on developing the writers of tomorrow, offering their knowledge and time, often in stressful working conditions and for very little pay, and in turn they get summers off to do more work—and it's not always their own. All this time they spend taking care of the future of others. The least we can do is lend a little support and inspiration to them.

Each year we are more connected than ever, and so much good has come out of it. Participants have written and sold books they have begun during the annual session. People have formed writers' groups—and friendships—out of it. There are some folks who return year after year just to have that moment of connection.

Look, even if what we write doesn't turn into a million-dollar book deal, there's something important about showing up for one another—and ourselves. If we reach out to others admitting our challenges while also cheering one another on, we're all capable of more than we expected. Those 1000 words come easier when you feel supported.

It is with that enthusiasm that I have put together this book: a collection of the previously published emailed letters, along with new material from other authors and myself. My hope is that at any moment you could open these pages and know you're not alone in your creative life—and that yes, you can do the work.

WHY *1000* WORDS, THOUGH?

I'm a *New York Times* bestselling author who has written seven books of fiction and one memoir. My books have been translated into sixteen languages, and I have contributed work to practically every major publication in the US. I have a small home and a fat puggle and I live a quiet life in New Orleans that I've worked hard to achieve, and I built it all on my words. For two decades, I have been writing professionally and have thought long and hard about productivity, creativity, how the two are intertwined, and what works for me every day of the week.

Since I began writing books in earnest, I have used 1000 words a day as my regular writing goal. It's about four typed pages double-spaced. If I write 1000 words a day, five days a week, give or take time for edits, research, and other job responsibilities, I can finish a messy-as-hell first draft in about six months. It usually takes me another six months to get it in enough shape to be able to share it with other people.

The 1000 words (or whatever is comparable in your chosen genre) is a guideline. It's my personal guideline because it has worked for me. I have published a book every two years for the last eighteen years, so I stand behind this premise.

But 1000 words is more than just about writing to me. I see it as:

- a good day's work
- a meetable goal
- a step toward finishing a project
- a simple metric for creative output

It's both a quantifiable goal and an inspirational concept.

I know plenty of published writers who write far fewer words a day (and those who write far more!), and they produce what they need to produce either way. It's just a number, in the end. The last thing I want to do is slot people into an entrenched system that may not be healthy for everyone.

I can sit here and say that the word count matters, that the numbers matter, and they do. But what I'm really saying is that in terms of what we need or want to write, showing up matters, but having focus matters more. These letters, this structure, this encouragement and support, anyone can access it. Then all you have to do is sit down and write.

I think it's a solid goal to hit, 1000 words. I always feel satisfied at the end of the day when I see what I've written. Feeling satisfied is a valuable part of the process. Doing things that encourage ourselves to keep going—also part of the process. Setting reasonable but worthwhile deadlines for ourselves. Challenging ourselves to see what we can accomplish, what we're capable of. All of this is tied into the general concept of meeting a goal.

And that's essentially what I'm trying to do here: whatever they are, I want to assist you in reaching your writing or creative goals.

One thousand words helps me. I hope it helps you, too.

1

CHOOSING TO WRITE

WHY I WRITE

Why am I committed to this act in my life? These answers I have developed over time, and I imagine they could change, but I'm more than fifty years old, and there are some things I know to be true.

I write because it's the thing I have to offer, the sharpest skill I have. I write to make people feel less alone. I write as an act of service. I write because I want to communicate messages with the world. I write because it's a political statement, because I'm a feminist, and I want to exercise my freedom of speech. I write because I believe in myself, and that I have something worth saying. I write because I'm an artist, and if I didn't make my art I'd probably go mad. I write because it's fun; I take genuine pleasure in the words dancing before me on the page. I write to make myself laugh. I write to process my shit. I write because it's my job, and I get paid to do so, and I don't take that for granted. I don't take any of this for granted, ever.

And I write because I have mental health issues, and writing is one way I contend with my anxiety.

It never feels like anything important is real to me unless I've written it down in some way. Even if it's just in my journal, in secret, in hiding. My specific business or artistic dreams or goals operate right alongside this need to steady myself in the world with my words. How do I cut through all the constant buzzing around me and capture the simple truths? With the slash of a sentence.

WRITING IS FREE

You have everything you need to make your art every single day. You have a pen and paper or, if you prefer, your laptop. Some people like to use their cell phone. I have used all three of these things and sometimes, when I have nothing, I repeat an idea in my head until I can get to a place where I can write it down. Whatever works, use it.

Unlike many other forms of art, you don't need much physically to write. And you don't need an audience. You don't even need formal training. Though I did study writing as an undergraduate, I didn't get an MFA. After college, I didn't have access to the pathways of academia. I started out by writing little stories online and in my notebooks. I used to print them out at whatever temp job I was doing or at Kinko's. Then I would staple them into tiny books and sell them on the internet or at parties I threw, until finally I had written enough stories to form a book. I just had a lot to say. I genuinely didn't understand why people wouldn't want to do this all the time. Little arts and crafts projects.

If you have one hundred stories in your head or you have just one story bursting out of you, either way, you're all set. Writing is free for everyone. You can make whatever you want, wherever you want. You can make your own rules, your own universes, your own witty dialogue, anytime you like. It's free to entertain ourselves all the time. Aren't we lucky?

THE PLEASURES OF WRITING

The best part of being a writer is the actual writing and the community you build along the way. Commercial success, a good review, a cool book cover that everyone compliments, all the likes you get on a post—all of that feels good, all of that is important, because it's important to feel good and be recognized. But also, it's fleeting. In the long haul, those things are temporary, and it's the growth and joy of putting down the words on the page, the development of both the body of work and yourself as a person, in addition to the supporting of other people and being supported by them, that makes it all worthwhile. Those are things you can have every day of your life. They are all possible.

WHAT ARE YOU WAITING FOR?

"I've always wanted to write a book" is a thing people tell me all the time, and I fear I never respond to this as they would like me to, but I only know how to ask why they haven't yet. What are you waiting for?

Not a fair response to everyone, and not applicable to everyone, for some of us have plenty of things preventing us from tending to our creative work: life, family, jobs, outstanding college loans that insistently need to be paid, and health issues, physical and mental alike. Weekly T-ball games. That lawn won't mow itself, and trust me, it's past due. So I could ask you this question and you will have an answer immediately and then I will shut the hell up.

But there are others of you I could ask and you will say either wistfully or with perhaps a little embarrassment, "I know, I know." You are not making time for these important things: your work, your writing, your art, your creative self. This personal, intimate thing for you to call your own.

Now, I'm not raising my voice at you, but I am being direct and perhaps a little confrontational. You have something to say, you have some dreams of saying it. You know how to write, how to put one sentence after another, and you recognize the value of giving something a beginning, middle, and end. It's your story, or it's your grandmother's story, or it's a story you've made up from scratch. It hums around in your head. Maybe it even feels like it wants to claw its way out of you. You always saw yourself doing it, telling this story, but you never took that first step. Because.

Whatever the case, the words are in there, and you think about them all the time. Are you afraid to find out what will happen if you try to write them down? Do you fear the work you will have to do? Are you concerned about having to approach the particular kind of truth that can come only when one sits alone with their mind and their words? Are you a coward? (I don't think you are.)

My friend the writer and filmmaker Priyanka Mattoo waited years before she started writing her memoir because "My fear was always I love books so much that if I'm bad at writing I will have to die." But then she realized, "If I die and haven't written a book, well, I'm dead anyway. Might as well have tried."

What if you went your whole life without knowing if you could have done this? Are you letting this aspect of yourself—your creative goals—pass you by? Can you see how this would be a special opportunity for you, to try to write whatever it is you want to write? What are you waiting for?

WHAT IF WE HAVEN'T WRITTEN IN A WHILE?

Here are three reasons why we might stop writing:

1. It's a planned break for either professional or creative reasons.
2. Life happened. An emergency or undeniable distraction has taken our writing time away from us for longer than we would like or expected, and now we are having trouble getting back into it.
3. We stopped years and years ago. We gave it up, as if we moved to a new city away from an old friend, and as the years passed, we lost touch with it, but we always missed it, and we never forgot it. Our old writing friend.

No matter how long it's been since you've been apart from your work, it can feel like forever. If you take a week off, if you take two months off, or a year, or if you haven't written since college. It feels hard to get back into it. The words feel foreign on the page. Do these sentences even make sense? Are these even words? What *are* words anyway?

Every single time getting back into writing after a break is frustrating. Every single time. There's never a moment I step effortlessly into my work again. There's never a day where I just slide back inside my writing like I'm putting on a silk robe. It's clunky and it's hard and it usually requires carbohydrates, and I'm in a foul mood for at least a day, if not two. Ask all my friends.

It's an issue for every writer I know: How do we reclaim our connection to our work?

Honey, don't worry, you got this.

All you have to do is find your place at the beginning. You don't even have to write the thing you want to write. You just have to write *about* it. Write a little letter to yourself. Sit down somewhere quiet. Tell yourself why you want to write it, what you think it can be, why you dream of doing it, why this pen feels good in your hand, why this notebook looks nice on your table, why this stolen moment you claim for yourself is important, how it felt the last time you wrote, however long ago it was, and how it feels to be back at it again, here with yourself and your brain. Start there, and see what happens next.

YOU CAN BE ANYWHERE
AND WRITE THESE WORDS

Before I wrote my first book twenty years ago, I had a vague idea that I would eventually write one. I was writing all the time, stolen moments in cafés or on the subway, early in the morning, late in the evening, constantly churning out words. I couldn't quite see that I was in the process of writing something that would eventually become a book. I was occasionally getting essays published, and I had put out a few zines of short stories, one with a small press. I had words bursting out of me. I only needed a place to put them.

A friend of mine said to me, "Why aren't you writing a book yet? It's time." And then she offered me an opportunity: a place to live for the summer, a small cottage in Northern California on her boyfriend's land. He had a dog that needed long walks—a big dog, a Tibetan mastiff. I saved up enough money from all my freelance jobs and headed west.

Every day I walked the big dog and I wrote 1000 words. I also drank a lot of cheap, cold white wine and ate too much pasta and read dozens of books, and I had several miniature nervous breakdowns because I was by myself so much, and also because I was getting rid of all this emotional stuff by writing this book, stuff I hadn't known was there but now it was out, and it was on the page, 1000 words at a time.

I got up every morning and did it. I figured I would never have this amazing gift of time and space again. If I didn't write this book now, then when would it happen? In the fall I would go back east, where I would crash on a friend's couch for a while and return to work, to a contract job I hated. What if I had nothing to show for this summer?

At the end of the three months, I had an extremely rough first draft of a book. Whatever was going to happen next, at least I had done it. I had no idea what I was doing after that moment. But I had made this thing that was all mine.

Eight books later, I've learned a few things. You don't need it to be summer, and you don't need to be in a cottage in the woods. You can be anywhere and write those words. You just have to want it.

You can create a sense of isolation in your mind. You can tap into that hunger and desire to make something new. It's all sitting right there. A pen, some paper, and your brain.

THE SHIP

Let's say the work is the ship.

And let's say the ship needs to sail from one shore to the other. You start on one side, you make it all the way across a huge body of water, and then you can dock that ship. (And hopefully that body of water really represents something between 65,000 and 85,000 words.) But that's the journey: one shore, over the water, to the other shore.

Now, let's say you get a third of the way across that body of water and you suddenly lose wind and your sails flutter and then flop. Or let's say when you're almost halfway to the shore you realize you were reading the map incorrectly; you can still change course to get you where you need to be, but it's going to add a little time, make the trip a little longer. Or maybe you get three-quarters of the way, to where you can nearly see the shore in the distance, and then the least helpful member of your writing group says, "Wow, this is one dumb ship. I can't even believe you thought you could sail it in the first place."

Resist the urge to abandon the ship. I repeat—do not abandon the ship. Do not get on that little lifeboat and paddle back to shore. Do not get depressed and drink a bottle of rum and then jump overboard. Do not radio for help and get airlifted home and then apply to law school instead.

Just make it to the shore. That's all you have to do. Then you can examine the ship for holes and dents and damages. Then you can see if the ship is worth sailing again. But get to the other side first. The wind will come back. Perhaps you will have to paddle. But you must try to get there. Otherwise, you'll be wondering forever what could have happened. Otherwise, you'll never know what the other side of that body of water looks like. Because I promise you, it's a beautiful view.

HOW TO BEGIN

Sometimes we begin with a voice in our head, a character speaking to us. Sometimes we begin with a big (or little) idea that we can't seem to stop thinking about or shake. Sometimes we begin with a personal tragedy, and sometimes we begin with something that makes us laugh or turns us on.

We think: I can write this.

We stack the pens and pluck out our favorite notebook from the stack and download some new albums.

I often feel light-headed. Buoyant and available and game. There's this feeling of falling in love with something new.

With every project we are learning how to write again. We are convincing ourselves we can do it. We are writing letters to ourselves in our journals like incantations. We commit to an idea; we commit to ourselves. Here we go again. A new project. A new me.

And then we sit down. We start at the beginning. There is no wrong path, because we always must write through the mistakes to find the solutions. It's impossible to go in the wrong direction, because when we start a new project, any way we go is the right direction. We just have to know that we want to write.

You are here for a reason! Now begin.

2
THE SEASONS

We develop a regular writing practice because it's the surest and most direct way to get any real work done. One thousand words a day: it feels logical and precise and orderly. But the creative life cycle is year-round, and it operates in ebbs and flows. Sometimes our process is quieter and more intimate, and sometimes we are productive and streamlined and the words flow noisily and easily. Summer is usually my most productive time in terms of generating new work and getting words down on the page. For you, it might be at a different time, or in multiple, shorter spurts throughout the year. But since for most of us the writing process involves different phases, I have found it helpful to think of them in terms of seasons.

Winter is an internal and developmental phase. It's when we ask ourselves questions to develop our baseline creative self. Like: How do you view yourself as an artist and a writer and a creative person in the world? What are your desires? What do you want to get out of your work? What does it mean to you to do work? What are the goals—both big and small—you hope to accomplish? How do you feel about the story you have to tell? Winter is the time to be thoughtful, self-interrogative, and centered. Now we begin to understand why we've chosen to write.

Spring is about prepping for our project, assessing what we need in order to move forward and be as productive as possible. It's a moment to examine what our distractions are, how sometimes they are out of our control, but also how sometimes we create them for ourselves. And to notice if we're talking ourselves out of progress—or even getting started in the first place. How do we get out of our own way so we can succeed? And how do we plan for the future of our work? How do we give ourselves all the care and thought we need to be ready to write? How do we situate ourselves in our world and then set ourselves up to write? How do we arm ourselves with what we need to proceed? In spring, we contemplate productivity and streamlining our process. It's a moment to be strategic, analytical, and pragmatic.

Summer is when we've carved out time in our schedules, we've plotted out the future, and we're ready to commit to generating new work. (This season is how all this began—with #1000wordsofsummer!) Let's get messy, let's make mistakes, let's write into all of it with abandon and see what we can create. We're in the rhythm now, so how do we ride our momentum to the end? Ever so slightly we contend with where this is all going, but mostly we write with pure joy.

And finally, **fall** is when we acknowledge the need to give ourselves grace. We do not accomplish work all the time. If we flowed in summer, perhaps now we need to ebb. How do we not judge ourselves when we need a break? How can we recognize when we need to pause and regroup? We need to remember the words will always be there for us, no matter what.

Figuring out how to move through our process efficiently, honestly. Contending with the hard stuff of life and recognizing it doesn't have to derail our work. These are our challenges. But always remember the pleasure of the act of writing—the magic of inventing new ideas and worlds—and move toward that. There's always a way to get there again. Season after season.

ABOUT THE LETTERS

After I finished the fifth year of #1000wordsofsummer, I sat down and reread all the letters from the authors who had generously agreed to contribute their words to this project. What I saw was a time capsule of life in America between 2018 and 2022, the moments of the personal and the political, not to mention a global health crisis. Our structures were taxed—in particular, our families. And a reinvention of how we work in the world today. Some of these letters serve as a reminder of those times and what we lived through.

Witness, for example, Melissa Febos taking early-morning runs to maintain her sanity during the early days of lockdown in New York City. Or Liz Moore and Courtney Sullivan talking about the struggles of parenting and writing during the pandemic. Then there's Laila Lalami using writing as a respite and a distraction from the struggles of the world. And R. O. Kwon finding her way back to her practice through the development of an online writing group. I remembered again those times so vividly through their words.

And yet, what also emerged was the realization that the challenges, distractions, joys, and successes were both specific to these moments in time and not. Which is to say that while it was an extreme period of time in all our lives—and continues to be, in some cases—at any moment, the world can test us in brand-new ways and possibly impact our creativity and productivity. There is always a reason to not be writing, but there is also always a reason—and a way—to return to it eventually. If you are here now, it's because you're interested in finding that way.

One last note: these letters stay true to the authors' original texts, privileging their intended voices over stylistic consistency throughout the book.

3

WINTER

I find the idea of starting something new thrilling. I have learned to embrace the fear that comes along with it. Every time I sit down to begin a project, I always think about those people who go to Coney Island on New Year's Day—the members of the Polar Bear Club—for a swim. In the chilly sunshine, they rip off their clothes and run into the water. How do they find the courage? I'm sure they don't think about it too much. You just have to go for it. Don't psych yourself out. It's going to sting no matter what—but you'll feel great afterward.

When I start a book from scratch, not one page is typed. There are just a few ideas kicking around in my head, some handwritten notes. Usually there's this sort of vaguely plump feeling in my brain whenever I think about the characters, where they are, mixed with this hazy notion of their conflicts, external and internal both. I think: *How the hell am I going to do this again? Go from zero to hundreds of pages.*

But I've learned to transform the nerves into enthusiasm for the most part. My approach is "I get to write a novel" versus "I have to write a novel." And I think about what I desire. What kinds of stories I want to tell, what voices I want to give life to in the world.

You may be starting a new project, too. Now might be a good time to explore why you want to write it and what kind of writer you want to be.

And there may be some of you who are trying to finish long-term projects. Dusting off drafts that have been sitting in drawers or trying to push through to the end of something you've been toiling on for years. This book might feel heavy in your mind. There are all kinds of feelings already attached to this work from your personal history. You may be thinking to yourself: Why haven't I finished this already?

Don't talk yourself out of it. Ask yourself instead: Why do I want to finish it?

Whatever happened before this moment is irrelevant. We tear off our clothes and race down the sand to the icy cold water. We embrace the sting. To show ourselves we can. We start anew on our work, together. We just have to try.

I believe in you. You can do this. Now let's begin.

FOUR TRUTHS

1. We can't finish what we don't start.
2. The only way to the end is through.
3. It's important to celebrate our accomplishments.
4. We must forgive ourselves for that which we have simply not done yet.

WHAT DO THE WORDS DO FOR YOU?

The words do so many different things for people. If your writing is for comfort, let it comfort you. If your writing is for process, let it be for process. If your writing is to change your life or even the world, let that change roll. If your words are a war cry, for the love of God, please *howl*.

I know what the words do for me: for an hour or two, when I write, it's a place I can go to feel safe. It has always worked that way, ever since I was a child. The safety of a sentence. The sensation when I push and play with the words is the purest I will ever feel. The calm space of my mind. I curl up in it. I love when sentences nudge up against each other, when I notice a word out of place and then put it in its correct spot. I can nearly hear a click when I slot it into place. I love making a sentence more powerful, more dramatic or moving or sad, and I love when I make a sentence quiet enough that I can almost hear the sound of my own breath. More than anything, I love when a sentence makes me laugh.

The words light up on the page, showing me what to do, where they want to go. They have always been my best friends in the world. All I need is for a few of them to show up. To soothe me.

Yes, yes, it's different for everyone—but we're all still here together. I can only speak of my particular intimacy and hope to connect with you. That's what writing is: our particular intimacies. I offer up the idea of the safety of a sentence for you right now, the possibility of a place to put yourself, to put your heart. A place to rest for a while from these feverish days.

Today, before you begin your writing, think about this question: What do the words do for you?

YOUR STORY IS WORTH TELLING

I have written one memoir, and before I began I had to ask myself, truly, if my story was worth telling. We all wonder sometimes if our story is worth telling. If it's worth writing those 1000 words, let alone seventy thousand of them. I can't tell you what the reader will think of your story, but I can suggest a reframing of your narrative of the writing of it.

Stop thinking of it as the story of you and instead start thinking of it as the story you have to tell. How can you, in the writing of it, make it interesting? What will your approach be that will make it feel different or special? Will it be in an innovative structure? Will it be in the most gorgeous, breathtaking language? Will it be in the timing of it all, where you sink emotional moment after emotional moment? Will it be written in a hooky, addictive, page-turning style? Will it be rich with captivating cliff-hangers? How can you tell it in a way that has never been told before? How can you write a wholly unique story?

Life is a series of moments, some bigger, some smaller, and that's it. You can hang them together like forgotten Christmas lights left up year-round; or like beloved memorabilia secured on a refrigerator, maybe a postcard from long ago or a photo booth strip; or like flyers tacked to a community board in a café, advertising services or looking for lost dogs; or like signs promoting opposing local candidates stuck side by side in competition on neighbors' front lawns; or like drying clothes pinned to a line, flapping in the wind beneath the sunshine. Your job is to arrange these moments into a beautiful or captivating or intriguing display.

Stop thinking of it as your life. Start thinking of it as a story. Your story will be interesting because of *how you tell it.*

ROXANE GAY

One of the greatest gifts you can give yourself as a writer is to take yourself seriously. This does not mean you should take yourself too seriously, but it does mean that if you love writing, if you put in the work of writing, you are a writer. You don't need to ask anyone if you can call yourself a writer. You don't need to reach a certain publishing thresh-old. So long as you put pen to paper or fingers to keyboard, you are a writer.

And if you are a writer, you want to respect your craft the same way you respect the other important things in your life. Make time for your writing, whether it's writing itself, reading, participating in the literary community, or anything else that contributes meaningfully to your creative life. Write regularly, which does not mean you need to write every day but does mean that your work will be stronger if you are consistent. When you make a time to write, honor that com-mitment to yourself and your creative work as much as you honor all the other commitments in your life.

I am also a big believer in not diminishing our writing. So many writers will talk about their writing in the most dismissive ways. They'll say they "wrote a thing," or offer a

1000 WORDS

few self-deprecating words before sharing a new publication. Sure. Most of us deal with low self-esteem, but if you're taking yourself seriously as a writer, you need to believe your writing deserves to be treated with respect and care. You don't need to be arrogant but it's okay to be proud. Writing takes effort and time and imagination. It's okay to acknowledge that you're invested in your craft. It's okay to give a damn about your writing. And yes, if such is the case, it's okay to be confident. When you write something that's great, own that. Say that. Those moments of confidence can be painfully fleeting. Enjoy them while you can.

Here's the thing . . . making yourself or your writing smaller doesn't make anyone like you more, I promise you. So today, you're writing 1000 words. And you will write many more words after that. Those words will matter. They may not change the world, but they will change you.

VALUING YOUR CREATIVITY

It's important to value your creative self and what it can give you. I don't think you can be your best without that. We love our friends, we love our family, our partners, too: there is a system of mutual support there. We need these relationships to be healthy and whole. But to feel fulfilled we also need our relationship with our creative self to be healthy. We do this by paying attention to the conscious choices we make to benefit our ideas and artistic output and to what we gain from producing our work. We won't be as happy as we could be without engaging with that side of ourselves.

I'm always excited about witnessing how the creative mind works, both in myself and in my peers. How it solves problems even when we aren't necessarily thinking about them. And how it operates beyond our conscious control to give us what we need. It's intimate, the relationship we have with our creative self. It's purely for us and no one else.

Your creative self is composed of your brain, your heart, and your time. To protect your creativity, you must tend to them all.

The creative self looks out for us—if we look out for it. If we do our work, invest our time in ourselves and our art and our imagination, keep our mind clear for stretches of time just to rest it, balance ourselves between blankness and stimulation, get enough sleep, read, write, think. If we honor that thing that provides us with so much, it just might help us out one day. After the rain stops, it shows up. Quietly slips a solution to a plot problem into your head, for example, and cracks open the narrative of your book. Makes us feel good and sunny and proud and able to communicate with the world.

Are you caring for yourself—the deep, intimate creative self? Are you giving it the nurturing it deserves? The goal is to always be getting closer to the creative self.

Respecting your creativity is respecting yourself.

OUR PROCESS TAKES MANY FORMS

Not every moment of our lives is meant to be productive in a quanti-fiable way. I know this to be true because I have seen it time and again in my own life. When I think I'm not doing any work at all because I can't see the evidence in the form of a word count. There's no way I'm moving forward right now, I think, because hello? I'm obviously sitting still.

A helpful thing to remember is that our process takes many forms. Reading a book is part of the process. Exchanging ideas with a writer friend or an advisor of some kind is part of the process. Researching a time in history. ("What the hell was going on in 1975?" is definitely a question I have spent an afternoon with.) Listening to music you think your character might like. I have spent hours searching vintage cloth-ing online that I thought a character might wear. Taking long walks to clear your head is part of the process. Those morning stretches, that thirty-minute jog at dusk. Meditation. A chicken-scratch idea on a Post-it Note that doesn't go anywhere at all. Even if you never look at that note again, it can be part of your process.

Winter is tough for some of you out there, I know. Sometimes the struggle is as simple as missing the sun on your bones. If you're working your way through something right now, it might be helpful to acknowledge the things you're doing that *are* benefiting your work, even if the words aren't showing up just yet. Maybe make a list of the things you can do, are doing to benefit your mind and your creative process. It will all add up to something positive eventually. I promise if you are engaging in a curious life, only good can come out of it.

I think a lot about how easy it is to get stuck in the quicksand of life. I'm interested in it not only from a personal perspective but also a writing perspective. A stuck character, trying to unstick themselves. How people can get trapped by happenstance or bad luck. Things outside their control. Just a few wrong moves. A loss of momentum. No one's fault, a lot of the time, this stuckness. Except when, a little bit, it is.

In my real life, I see this particular state of being as a cautionary tale. How easy it would be to tread water a little longer. How easy it would be to just sink into the earth a little more. At any moment any of us could give in to it. Not just in our writing but in our lives.

That's why we have to remember to do all these things to take care of ourselves.

Read, walk, breathe, think.

BRYAN WASHINGTON

A recurring question in my writing centers around "value."
It's pretty annoying. Wondering "why" my words and interests could possibly "matter" to a reader takes up a lot of real
estate in my process. But it's a *question* and not a *problem*
because, like a lot of writing advice, it's ephemeral; you
can change the answer if you want to (consequently, most
writing advice is literal bullshit; I'm allergic to giving it and I
generally don't).

It's a canonical "who cares." The concern simply changes
forms, accelerating exponentially in the last week/month/
year alone. But, lately, I've wondered if this isn't a good thing:
maybe, as we change, along with our loves and distresses and
hopes and humors, our framework for what we prioritize on
the page changes, too. Our language(s) grow alongside us.
Our vernaculars expand to encompass our entire selves, however varied or paradoxical or scary that may feel. Maybe this
dynamism is simply the business of being a person; putting it
on the page is another way of taking up space.

In this way, the question of *voice* actually becomes one
of *agency*. It can be difficult to trust yourself! Doesn't matter
whether you're writing your first 1000 words or editing the

final 1000 in your contracted hexalogy. It can be tough to sit in the knowledge that the work that most sustains us—the strange, wonky, deeply unmarketable thing—could actually be the work *for* us. If you aren't a straight, wealthy, white cis-dude, the bulk of Western culture is architected to convince you otherwise. All the same, the hardest person to convince can be yourself.

So, I'm going to break my rule and offer some advice: trust yourself. Give yourself grace. Trust yourself to know that there's value in your interests. Trust yourself to know that your being interested in X gives it value. When we put love in our work, it becomes palpable. A tangible thing. One word follows the next, until you're gifted with a page that's as much *for* you as it is *of* you. And then you'll keep going. The rest of us are excited to meet you.

MAKE A CHOICE

We often wonder how to know if we're making the right choice creatively when there are so many possibilities. I understand fear. I understand caution. But at some point, we must shake off the indecision and just move forward with our work. Choose your project. Choose your sentences. Choose your ideas. Choose your ending. It's your trip and no one else's.

If your biggest dream was to write for television, you wouldn't say things like, "I should really write a television pilot." Instead you would say, "I'm writing a television pilot," and you would get up an hour earlier every day to work and you would lock yourself in your house on the weekends, also to work, and you would read those television writing books and you would buy that impossible software program and you would join a writing group or make friends with someone else who wanted to write for television and you would swap scripts and give each other feedback and go out and get drunk one night and toast each other for being brilliant (and maybe there would be some sort of awkward sexual chemistry between you but that's your business and not mine) and then you would try to find an agent and then who knows what happens next? But this would be you in fact *doing enough* to try to achieve this goal.

But what if you don't do it? Are you the kind of person who lives your life mired in regrets, or are you the kind of person who makes your decisions and moves on with them? Can you see the fact that you are not doing these things as choices you are making, to make room for the things you can and want to do? The people doing all the things you want to be doing—for the most part, no one is doing the work for them, no one is handing it to them on a plate.

Certainly, some of them have generational wealth or connections or are overachievers, but most of them are worker bees like the rest of us, buzzing about the giant hive of creativity. We cannot envy them for trying. We should look to them as role models, instead.

If you want something, do what it takes to get it. If you decide not to pursue a path, accept your choices.

SUSAN ORLEAN

I've been writing for a living my entire working life. I did
a brief stint waiting tables (something I think everyone
should do at some point in their life, for all the lessons you
will learn about time management, food, the treatment of
service people, and how to charm your way to better tips).
Other than that, all I've ever done is write. I feel unbeliev-
ably, wildly lucky to have had that be the case—what could
be better than to get to do the thing you want to do? But
I rarely pause and think about why I do it, and whether I
should do it, and what it means in an existential way. So now
and again, I force myself to take that pause and consider
what it is that I do and why I do it.

So why do I write? I love the pure experience of it. I
love making sentences that do what I want them to do. I love
the carpentry of the process, the cobbling together of words,
the sturdy little structures made when you line them up in
a solid way. On a bad writing day, it's easy to forget the en-
joyment of making sentences—how pleasing it can be when
it's going well. Reminding myself of that baseline pleasure is
a tonic when the more exasperating stuff crowds in (the sentence that just won't comply, the source who won't call you

back, the deadline that is causing you to panic, the editor who nitpicks). I need to reacquaint myself with the delight gotten from nailing a series of words in place that feel right.

Why else do I write? Well, I like telling people things. I like it very, very much. I have a bit of a missionary's zeal when it comes to passing along a story. I can savor things in private, but I really get excited when I have the chance to share a story. I love spinning out a string of funny anecdotes and interesting observations to an audience. Writing is a natural extension of that—or rather, a way to do that same storytelling to a bigger audience than, say, at a dinner party, namely, the world of readers. This urge dovetails with another critical part of why I write, which is that I like learning things. I am the most willing student in the world. The less I know about something, the more thrilled I am about learning it, and then, in turn, the more thrilled I am about telling other people about what I've learned.

I write because I think it's important. That's a broad statement, since there are a million different kinds of writing, but it applies to all of them. Writing in all its forms is the essence of human interaction. (It's interesting how the internet, which we all believed would be the end of writing, has instead made us all write all the time. If we're not tweeting, we're texting, or we're posting on social media, or . . .) Being able to communicate through writing is absolute magic: Little marks on a page or screen conveying knowledge! Emotion! Mystery! To make those little marks on the page for a living is a miracle.

What's the value of wondering why you write? Everyone benefits from stepping back and considering what and why they do what they do, whatever it is that they do. But it's particularly essential for writers to ask and answer that question. In truth, writing is *hard*. It can be discouraging, exhausting, frustrating, depleting. It is easy to forget why it's so compelling, why it's so satisfying, why it's so important, why and how it can feel good. Taking a moment to do that once in a while reboots that part of you that should write with passion and drive and a sense of delight. You should write with a burning desire to do it. You should write with urgency, with the feeling that you just *must* do it. Readers can sense that, just as they can sense when someone is merely shuffling words around, without feeling fired up about it. I like to picture myself tugging on the reader's shirtsleeve, shouting, "YOU JUST HAVE TO HEAR THIS!" I like to picture myself bubbling over with my story, as if I simply can't contain it; I must share it *or else*. When I can lock into that emotion while I'm working, I can answer the question of why I write very simply. I write because I must.

THE ABOUTNESS

This is something I think about all the time—do you? What my work is about. What I'm trying to say, what I'm trying to accomplish by writing it. Who I'm trying to talk to isn't necessarily what it's about, but it's helpful to imagine them sometimes; if you could picture what you're trying to say to a particular person or group of people, then perhaps it can help infuse your work with an aboutness.

I return to this question often as I'm writing. My notebooks are full of me querying myself. "What is this about? What are you trying to say here?" (Yes, I address myself in second person in my journal sometimes.) Some people know right away, those lucky bastards. They are maybe not born with an aboutness, but it can show up for various projects, dump itself on a writer like a perfect light rain in the summer heat, refreshing, delightful: here is an idea, fully formed, now run with it.

You have to keep chasing it repeatedly. Revising it. It's your throughline.

I've had ideas appear fully formed to me twice for long-form projects, and both times I wrote the book in record time. But otherwise: it takes forever.

Uncovering the aboutness can mean creating a document that will be in motion throughout the process. Here is what this project is about—or at least what I hope it will be about. It will require tweaks along the way but by the end it should be clear what the throughlines were all along. It's a document I can return to, as a resource, and as a stabilizing force. Another trail we can leave for ourselves.

Do you know what the throughlines are in your projects? Can you check in today? It's never a waste of time to tend to them. They can help you make your way through to the end of the book. No matter where you are in the process, your throughlines, and the development of them, are what hold your project together.

I'm always chasing the aboutness just like anyone else. It's elusive at times because we're always evolving. We're getting to know our characters, we're building out our theories, we've got research to do. We don't have all the answers right away. The characters or ideas are telling us something and forcing us to interact with them, figure out how to feel about them.

It's a kind of correspondence with yourself, writing something. By the end of your project, you'll know what it's about. And, in fact, that might be how you know you're done—when you figure out, finally, what it's all about.

MARIS KREIZMAN

At various times in my life, I was determined to write vampire erotica, a twisty thriller in the style of *Gone Girl*, or a chaste romance in which a nice Amish man removes a woman's bonnet but not her undergarments. All under a pen name, of course. I've been in and around the book publishing world for twenty years. I know what sells and I know how it's sold. I know so much about the system, so why wouldn't I try to game it? But wow, it turns out my vampires were bad at sex, and you could see my plot twists from a mile away.

I absolutely believe that writers should be more empowered. They should know more about the business of selling books in an industry that can so often feel opaque. But let's not worry about this right now. Because this is the good part. This is the time to dream, to pull out of your beautiful brain a sentence, a story, a world, that you are uniquely qualified to create. Let yourself dream.

When I sold my first book, a collection of essays about my disillusionment with the institutions I once believed in, my editor told me to forget all I knew about writing for publications with strict word counts. "You have no limits now," she said. "Write at whatever length you like. Don't be held back by constraints." How invigorating it felt to be free! And I want you to feel free, too.

There's time for cynicism later. This is your time.

So write the thing that you want to see in the world. You're the only one who can.

WHEN SOMEONE TELLS YOU NO

If we wait for someone to tell us yes, we will be waiting a long time. Doors do not open for us magically. The worst no I ever got was also the best no.

When I was twenty-one years old, a man considered to be an authority on literature suggested I not become a writer. It was a few days before I graduated from college. I was getting an undergraduate degree in creative writing. The visiting writer who had taught our senior fiction seminar told me, quite gently, to give up on my dreams.

I can picture so clearly that room where we sat together, him at a desk, sunlight streaming in from the windows behind him. He wasn't happy to see me when I walked in the door. I was young and punk and weird and had big hair. He would have been fifty-five that year. Bearded, gray, bespectacled. Seemed like one hundred years old to me, all-knowing, if a little disassociated from us all. His disconnection made us hunger for his praise all the more, I suspect. And he had already won the National Book Award by then; he was deeply entrenched in the literary world.

All semester, he had barely critiqued my stories, remaining quiet in class as my peers rattled off suggestions and ideas. He returned printouts of my work with just a few scribbles added. And now here I was visiting him in his office, ready for the moment where he would tell me . . . anything? Where I could improve, what opportunities he thought might exist for me. Truly, I would take all the help I could get.

His advice, however, was somewhat unexpected. He asked me what I wanted to do after graduation, and I told him I wanted to write. Without hesitation he said, "You know, honey, not everyone makes it as a writer." He suggested I could do other things involved with books. Perhaps become an editor or a publicist, both important jobs that require exceptional skills, smarts, and talent. But completely different jobs from the one I wanted.

I walked out of his office, dazed. I was discouraged. I suppose I had wanted him to say, "You're a genius. Let me make a few calls and get you an agent." But he was no career counselor, and what were any of us doing getting a degree in writing anyway?

Perhaps he thought I didn't have talent. Or, perhaps he saw me as frivolous. I was writing stories about sex and relationships and so-called domestic matters. He wrote big, sprawling novels that were about soldiers and war and violence. Maybe he didn't enjoy teaching, and this was a sloppy moment; he had never seemed excited to be there. To discourage someone from even trying, though? To say "give up" before I'd even gotten started?

Writing is holy, as my friend Patricia Lockwood says. It is true that it's hard to make it as a writer, or any kind of artist, for that matter. But if you love to write, you should write forever.

And I knew I could write. He was wrong. That much I knew. And I wanted to write. I had to assert that desire to myself in that moment.

For a long time, I used this story as inspiration for myself. He told me I couldn't, and yet somehow, I did anyway. He was an older man, negative and condescending. I'll show him, I thought. But it's only recently that I realized that moment was actually radically freeing. I was probably not suited to be a writer in the way he thought was important. But that didn't mean I wasn't suited to be a writer. In a way, he gave me a fresh start.

It's been nearly thirty years since that man told me I probably shouldn't bother. I'm old enough to realize that an important part of carving out your creative life is honoring your moments, your successes, no matter the size. And honoring the bad moments, too. Laying your burdens down. Building this writing life has always been about recognizing what was holding me back so I could move on. The visiting writer told me no. So I honor that rejection, I honor that moment. He said no, but I said yes.

SARA NOVIĆ

The literary world is big on advice. Because it's such a miry and solitary business, lots of beginning writers seek some confirmation that things get clearer as you go. Because it's such a miry and solitary business, lots of "established" writers love to give it, to feel that after spending big chunks of time alone in a room we might have some lessons of value to impart.

I get the appeal. I went to graduate school specifically to access this kind of knowledge. Now a writing workshop instructor myself, I've been known to wax on about craft, too.

But, dear writer, not all advice is good advice. Most importantly, not all advice is good advice for you. Have I tried waking up in the dark to write before the day begins because famous writers said I should? Of course. Did my Deaf ass have a complete freak-out about how I might never be able to write proper dialogue because Stephen King said writers should read their work aloud and listen to the cadence of their characters' conversations? You know it!

These tips work for lots of writers, but they certainly didn't work for me. And that's the real trick of it—finding your people, the ones who share your vision and help you get it across the finish line, instead of trying to drag it somewhere else.

I wrote parts of what would become my first novel while I was a college student. I cared a lot about the "rules" of writing because I wanted to get good grades and keep my scholarships, which are fine reasons to do something, but also have nothing to do with writing. The book came out all right, in the end. I felt I had given it my all; it was an important story to me, and a lot of readers enjoyed it.

But when it came time to write another book, those rules no longer applied. There were few books to look to as models for creating fully realized Deaf characters, and even fewer that engaged with the transformation of American Sign Language into two-dimensional form. To do it right, things were going to have to get weird.

Writing *True Biz* was hard, and the book did come out a little bit weird, and it was met with some resistance from some very smart people because of that. But it was also the book I wanted, and needed, to write. And in a real twist of fate, it turned out to be the book a lot of people needed to read.

Risk-taking doesn't always guarantee commercial success or even the structural integrity of a project holding together. Then again, if I'd stayed sitting at my desk trying to write like Stephen King, things definitely wouldn't have worked out. For everything there is a season: a time to listen to a brilliant writer friend or editor, and a time to rip out your (metaphorical?) hearing aids and do whatever the hell you want.

Today is a great day to do whatever the hell you want.

HOW TO KNOW IF YOU HAVE A GOOD IDEA

A good idea is one that you can't stop thinking about. Sometimes it keeps you up at night, as you think through every aspect of it, like you might with a crush. Or maybe you wake up first thing with it on your mind and you nudge it around gently in your brain, pushing and pulling parts of it back and forth, like ice plates in Antarctica, until some sort of beautiful ecosystem forms in your mind. Or you find yourself saying no to a night out with friends because you would prefer to stay home and work on the pages that have sprung forth from this good idea; and sometimes you get a little sweaty when you're working on it; and sometimes you feel a little sexy or horny, or sometimes you're absolutely starving, and the only thing that can feed you is this very good idea. It makes you feel fulfilled and alive in a brand-new way, and also possibly mildly obsessed (but not in an unhealthy way! In a totally fun way), and you figure out how to adjust your life around it a little bit on a regular basis. And then one day someone invites you to join a writers' group, or you see one advertised on a flyer at a local café, and even though it has never occurred to you to be in a writers' group, you do it, now you're in one. Or maybe you sign up for an open mic night at a bar or online, and you step forward, stand in the spotlight for a few minutes, just to see what it sounds like out loud, this good idea, and it turns out it sounds great. And you find your life has changed a little bit for the better all because of this idea, which turned out to be a good one, or at least good enough to make everything a little bit brighter and bolder in your world.

That's how you know it's a good one: when everything shifts.

GAINING CONTROL

—

Writing these 1000 words is an attempt to achieve a small semblance of control in our lives. To sit down and write is an act of grasping at a stable, realized moment in the whir of existence. It's a way to fix a feeling or a thought or a gesture in this particular moment in time. The questions and crises and doubts that filter through our days—this is how we capture them. Yes, we write toward the future, but also we claim right now with our words. One thousand of them, today.

WRITING COMPASS

Even though I allow myself to muddle around quite a bit while I write my first drafts, there's an intentionality to my work. To be more specific, there's a list of qualities a project must have before I fully engage with it.

My book must always have a strong, complicated female protagonist. It also must have a structure unique to anything I've done in my previous works; I always want every novel to feel new and inventive, even if there are common themes that linger from book to book. To create characters that feel imperfect and flawed but also worth loving or at least knowing. To invent a story that surprises and entertains. To be funny. To be honest. To do cartwheels with my sentences, but in a perfectly straight line. Showmanship and pleasure and emotional truth. The heightening of the intimate and the universal. All important to me. And finally, there has to be an element of compassion to the work, which is to say I need to be able to approach it from a compassionate place, explore the theme through the actions of the characters, and invite the reader to contemplate the idea of compassion themselves.

In a sense these are my writer's ethics. I know that if I'm abiding by them, I can feel free to move on with a project. Together, they are my compass.

Do you have your own list? Do you have an understanding of your aesthetics and desires? It changes, it evolves, I know. It's worth checking in every so often. Connecting with yourself so that your work can connect better with others. Write that list if you have a moment. The big picture of what you want to accomplish, the small ways to do it. What is your writing compass?

RUMAAN ALAM

Advice about writing is mostly pretty awful, but a long time ago, another writer said something to me—really an aside, a stray thought—that has stuck with me, as advice about writing or maybe advice about life itself. "No one is ever going to ask you to write a book," she said, and she'd know, having published three at that point.

I appreciate this statement because it's true; unless you're a disgraced politician or a famous celebrity, no one will ask you to write a book. (If you are a politician, no one will really read your book; if you are a famous celebrity, there are a million things more fun than writing a book that you could do.)

Take the "book" out of it; no one will ask you to write, full stop. It's up to you. You probably already knew that, which is why you're trying to produce 1000 words a day right now. Part of you knows that some percentage of those words won't be good, that you'll write and rewrite and revise and write more and slash and write more and revise and on and on. Yet without those first 1000 words, you have nothing, which is the first step of that proverbial one-thousand-mile journey.

No one is asking you to take that one-thousand-mile journey, not the way your dog asks you to take it for a walk, or your kids ask you for a snack, or your family or your work or the million demands of existence ask you for your attention. I find this liberating and hope that you will, too. Writing isn't something anyone wants from you but a thing you demand of yourself.

LAUREN OYLER

What is writing? How does it happen? Why do I do it? I have no idea. I have no set routine, or place, or time for writing; I often describe the experience of doing it as "torturous." Sometimes I imagine that if I had a routine it would feel less torturous, but I know that isn't actually true; it would just be torturous in a more comfortable chair. Whenever I finish something and read it over again the overwhelming feeling I have is distance: How did I write that? The only productivity trick I have is to maintain several projects at once so that my dread of working on all of them sends me to another secret project that I actually want to be working on but am not supposed to, because it distracts me from the more pressing obligations, which I allow to persist long after they need to in order to keep me from enjoying writing the secret project that I actually want to be working on. With every new piece or book, I always imagine that this time I'm going to figure out what I'm going to say and how I'm going to say it before I actually start, but so far that has never worked. (I think it's another procrastination tactic.)

What I take from this is that some uncertainty, discomfort, and, yes, distance is essential—that I need to feel like

I'm looking for something in my own mind. "The writer must not really know what he is knowing, what he is learning to know when he writes, which is more than the knowing of it," Joy Williams writes in "Uncanny the Singing That Comes from Certain Husks." "A writer loves the dark, loves it, but is always fumbling around in the light." This is why the best and only advice I can ever really give is, unfortunately, some version of the Nike slogan. At some point I get fed up with my anxiety or my other deadlines or my sense that the conditions for writing aren't right, and just . . . you know. It's helpful to remember that the ideal form of the book you're writing doesn't already exist somewhere out there for you to find. However it turns out is something you control—even if you open your project and have no idea how it got there.

WHEN TO WRITE ABOUT SOMETHING PERSONAL

There is a real value to time and reflection. How I feel about something in the moment is surely different in retrospect. There is something to be said for the purity of the instant response, of course, that flash of hot fire and emotion. But I prefer looking at an incident in the rearview mirror rather than in the middle of the intersection.

I'm thinking of an essay that took me four years to write. It's about something bad that happened a long time ago, but it's also about the state of America now, and it's also about the eternal state of being a woman. At some point I realized I was far enough away from the moment to have the right perspective to tell it.

I attempted to write the story so many times over those four years, and each time it turned out differently. Just the act of writing it in the first place, deciding this was a story worth telling, that it was important to me, was a specific version of it. In subsequent drafts I began to look at things from different angles than just the version I had been telling for most of my life. How did that one incident impact my actions later? How did I see things outside of my world connecting with it emotionally, aesthetically, metaphorically? Who was I thirty years ago and who am I now? I was slotting in different pieces from the past and present, letting in different shards of light until the whole piece was aglow.

If I had published the first version of it, or the second, or the third, the essay would not have been a lie, but it would not have been fully realized. If I had written it thirty years ago, it would have been raw and vulnerable and thrilling even but not aged correctly. I needed to spend enough time with it to see all the sides of it. And there could be even more sides, surely! But I have chosen this version as the one I'm going to tell.

I approached the writing with rigor, I worked the words repeatedly.

I had patience. Sometimes we must have patience. I circled the ideas and substance of the piece with deep consideration. If I am to tell this story, I must tell it with wisdom. I have lived a long time already. Have I not acquired some wisdom along the way? Best not to waste it.

The essay eventually became the cornerstone of a book proposal. At the time I was writing it I didn't know why I was writing it or what I would do with it. It was just one story in my life I was rewriting again and again for no reason at all except that I had thoughts and feelings and needed a place to put them. "They'll be safe there," I thought. They'll be safe in the document. I locked the words away until they were ready to show to the world.

Sometimes we write in the heat of the moment. We do not take care with our words. We write to process our feelings. That is an immediate benefit to writing. It's therapeutic as hell, writing. But we do not always need to publish these thoughts. They can exist, still, without anyone seeing them. I remind myself of this all the time. I didn't always know it. I had to learn that lesson, and occasionally I have to relearn it. It's so easy—too easy, perhaps—to publish our words for anyone to see. A pause, I suggest, for all of us. A breath here and there, before we hit send.

EMMA STRAUB

I am writing this from the middle of my book tour—well, the last day of the first leg of my book tour, the first time I've toured in person since 2016. This might seem odd, but what I wanted to write to all of you wonderful people about is not writing fiction but the writing I've been doing on the road—keeping a tour newsletter/blog. What to call it? It certainly contains no news. Mostly it contains pictures of people and food and sights and bookstores. Sometimes my face but mostly not.

My new book takes place partially in 1996, the year that I was sixteen, and people have been asking me a lot about research. Ha! I want to say, but they are serious. Because suddenly, 1996 is categorized as historical fiction; suddenly, 1996 is ancient and dusty. My answer to those people is that my only research was cracking open my diaries, of which there are many. In fairness, the diaries are ancient and dusty on the outside, but on the inside, they are alive, they are wild, they are all over the place and filled with poems and phone numbers and notes to my friends.

I still keep a diary, but now my diary is mostly about concrete things—what I saw, what I did, who I did it with. Not much room for six pages of wild feelings, which is about what

I did every day in high school, just reams of paper filled with every feeling and sensation running through my brain and body.

Part of it is that I know myself better now (this is what I tell myself) but part of it also is time—in 1996, my only telephone was a landline, and my only internet was AOL Instant Messenger, which I used sparingly. I used to have hours every day in which I had to entertain myself, and now that I am on tour, I find that those hours still exist, when no one else needs anything from me, and it feels a little bit like finding a lost treasure. There are more hours in the day.

I go home tonight and will be plunged back into my normal life and routine, with all the responsibilities that my life comes with nowadays. What I will miss the most is not the exciting meals in new places or even the beautiful bookstores filled with readers. What I will miss the most is that strange collection of hours in the middle of the afternoon, like an unexpected late beam of sunlight, that invited me to just slow down and stay awhile and notice what was around me. That is the part of being a writer that I rush through most often—that glorious part that I think all of us had as youths, when we could fill a notebook with our thoughts about ourselves and our friends and our lives, examined on the most microlevel. I invite you to do it with me, as much as you can. Let's curl up in the sunlight together and write in our diaries, knowing that noticing leads to more noticing, that paying attention to the worlds within us and outside of us fuels everything. The rest of our lives can wait, at least sometimes.

CHRISTOPHER GONZALEZ

Of all the questions I get asked about my writing, two are the most common: "How much of it actually happened?" and "How did you start writing fiction?"

To which I usually respond:

1. All of it's true; none of it happened.
2. I am a failed essayist.

Lately, I'm not excited about documenting the narrative reality of my own life. It's all fairly mundane. I wake up most mornings groggy and irate about the world, tend to my nine-to-five job out of obligation and financial need, and then, if I'm lucky, I might spend time with friends, drinking, laughing, sometimes crying. Mostly, though, deep pockets of my day are devoted to swapping tweets and TikToks or bonding over little heartbreaks in bubbled chat boxes. Wash, rinse, pop a melatonin, and repeat.

When I write, I'm searching for meaning in all this bland everydayness. This fog of "same same, dear God, it's all the same."

I choose fiction because with it I am able to crack the mundane wide open beneath a microscope. I can study its pulsing threads, the connective tissue between seemingly isolated events that have occurred across my life. They are the thorny bits that stick to the back of my brain or lodge themselves painfully in the fibers of my heart. I tweeze them out and begin the process of fabrication, expanding upon fact-checkable truths. I smudge and blur; I obfuscate. I create pathways for my characters where in real life I only remember a dead end. I step into the space of what-ifs and what-might-have-beens, navigating alleyways I'd never dare go down but now find myself braver, bolder. I confront past heartaches and loneliness and longings and despairs to find joy. Real joy.

I suppose I'm saying that writing gives me a second chance to live unfettered by insecurity or self-doubt. To do away with years of regret. To manage an anxious brain that never stops rattling. It's not about catharsis or suppression; it's about embracing all the mucky parts of myself, holding myself steady when the world feels anything but.

Writing keeps me going.

SHIFTING YOUR UNIVERSE

Writing allows you to shift your universe every day, in at least one small way.

It's about making a movement from one place to the next. The number is important, of course. The number is something quantifiable. "How did I do today? Well, I got my work done. I wrote this many words."

But I think things got easier once I began to understand that the word count was just a measure of the time and space available to me on the page. And in that time and space, a shift was possible every time I sat down to write.

Even just one beautiful scene. One thousand words offered enough room to describe a place or a person, maybe there'd be some chitchat, and for something else to happen. A choice to be made, possibly. An entrance, an exit. For someone to lift a large object over their head and decide which direction they want to throw it. For someone to see someone else—or themselves—in a new light. For someone to decide they didn't love somebody anymore. If they ever did in the first place.

What could I make happen during 1000 words? Which way would I nudge the universe? Even with all the mistakes I made on the page during that first rough draft, all the imperfect sentences and ideas, there was still a small push I could give to the story.

And in that shift on the page, there is always a shift in myself. There is a before the words and an after the words. I'm different because I made this world of words different. It may not always be clear to me exactly how. Each book I write is an accumulation of small shifts. But I know enough by now to trust that I will always come out the other side different than when I started.

BENJAMIN PERCY

It begins with a glimmer. Maybe I overhear a conversation in a bar. Maybe I pause on a certain, curious detail in the Sunday paper. Maybe I wake up with a dream still churning in my open eyes. I then rush to jot down the idea before it . . . evaporates. If you say to yourself, "I need to remember this later," you won't. So I send myself an email. Or I scratch something down on a napkin. Or I rip out an article with my notes scribbled in the margins. I harvest these glimmers. And pin them up in my office, near my desk. So that I flirt with them daily. And eventually—sometimes weeks later, sometimes months or even years later—a few of them glow brightly, and I realize how they are connected and they come together like a constellation. And I get to work. Often (especially if it's a novel) I outline. Sometimes (especially if it's a short story or an essay) I allow myself to be more impressionistic, chasing a voice, an image. But I always know my endgame. Always. Because when I know my end, everything in the story is building toward that moment, the paragraphs and chapters transferring their momentum, crashing forward like so many dominoes. People are sometimes afraid of the blank page. But if you know your end, even when you're starting from scratch, there is no blank page. The finish line is in sight—you just have to race to get there.

LEAH JOHNSON

When I began writing fiction, I was under the impression that there was something fixed and precious about the writing process. That—once I'd finished my MFA and my first manuscript—I would know exactly what it took to do so again and again. Mornings, not nights. Tea, not coffee. Pantser, never a plotter. And yet, my second novel couldn't be written at night. My third novel called for espresso, not tea. My middle-grade book needed to be tightly plotted and carefully planned. With each book, with each iteration of myself and career, my process continues to shift.

I'm no longer interested in waiting for the magic bullet—the one almighty answer from the literary gods that dictate The Way to write a novel. The work will evolve as I do, as will how I approach it. It's okay to give yourself over to the not-knowing. The I'm-still-figuring-my-shit-out. The maybe-this-never-gets-easier. There's a lot of room for play in those empty spaces between what we know and what we have yet to learn.

TELL THE TRUTH

No matter what you are writing—fiction, nonfiction, otherwise—you must give yourself permission to write it all down in an honest way. You must be courageous and tell the truth, whatever that truth means for you. Don't worry what anyone else thinks while you're in this precise act of generating new work. Don't let anyone else get in your head. You only have this one moment of pure creation. Use it to tell the truth.

THERE IS ONLY ONE YOU

We all question our work, how we write it, and the validity of its substance. More often than not I look at what I've written and think, "Well, this is obviously not very good!" But I trust that it will get there. I trust that the core me contains a message worthy of being spoken. I trust that if I write and rewrite and think and rewrite and stare out the window and read other people and then write and rewrite some more, it will get better. And then, maybe, I will be ready to be heard.

There is only one you, your voice is singular, and if you do not write these 1000 words no one will ever know what you have to say. You absolutely must have faith in yourself, that what you need to talk about is important, and that a reader will care about it. And you will write those 1000 words so that people will listen to you. You have go into this believing you are worth being *heard*.

WRITING INTO THE SHAME

Mostly I write novels, which can be emotionally honest, but are also inherently a lie. When I wrote my memoir, I decided to try to tell the truth about myself. Warts and all, I warned myself. Samantha Irby told me that whatever I wrote, I needed to be prepared for anyone in my world to have read it, that they would suddenly know these things about me, even the checkout guy at the grocery store. Rosie Schaap told me I needed to write myself as the biggest jerk in the book. I needed to be unafraid of questioning my role in certain situations in my life. I had to accept responsibility for my actions and be honest about my struggles.

So, I went into it with an open heart but also a critical eye toward myself. I had done things wrong. (We all have.) I had screwed up. I had been in unsafe situations. I had had to ask for help. Some of these things weren't bad, just vulnerable. But I needed to face all these moments.

In particular, I had trouble writing about a tough time in my life, when I was grappling with housing instability. When I've written about it in the past, I had presented it as perhaps a worthy struggle, not one that I should be admired for but one that I accepted as part of the life of an artist. What I had never contended with before—not truly—was how it had made me feel, the tenderness and vulnerability, and how it altered my perspective and how I engaged with the world. I wasn't being as honest as I could be, because I had never asked myself to be.

I wrote into the shame. I wrote into the fear. I lived in that time again, reading what I had written about it years ago, and then cutting out parts of it, the bits that felt of false bravery, and then digging deeper into what remained. I made myself admit the truth. I don't think I could have done it at the time things were happening. I was too busy surviving. We're not always capable of being honest about ourselves in the moment.

But what was the point of writing a book of this nature if I couldn't push myself to open up those old wounds and bleed a little on the page?

The hardest part of looking back was the fear of lingering too long in the sadness of a particular moment. That's why I needed to feel safe enough to know I would be able to return to the present. Just because I was sad once does not mean I need to stay sad forever.

What makes you feel taken care of and secure and nurtured so you can put yourself in the space where you are capable of being honest and vulnerable in your work? What do you need to do to be able to scratch open that vein and allow yourself to access those feelings? Maybe it's a small embrace you give yourself, letting yourself know it's going to be all right, you're still here, still alive, with so many stories to tell.

MIRA JACOB

Can we talk for a moment about expiration dates? The little
invisible stamp we all carry in the lining of our foreheads
that tells us that our time is running out, or just ran out, or
ran out so long ago that there is nothing we can possibly
write to make up for the literary life that might have been?
Because I have a feeling about expiration dates for dreams
in general (they're bullshit) and writing dreams in particular
(THEY'RE BULLSHIT).

I say this as someone who managed to publish fuck all
in her twenties and thirties, despite writing a few excellent
stories and many okay ones. As someone who by age thirty-
six worked from 9:00 a.m. to 9:00 p.m., with a short break
around dinnertime to feed a baby and stare at ~~the abyss~~
Facebook, where one endless 5 Under 35 list stared back
at me. As someone who wrote a novel from 11:00 p.m. to
1:00 a.m. for twelve years, which started to feel like a willful
self-delusion by year seven because why on earth was I
going on with my silly sentences when the world had clearly
passed me by?

I think about this all the time now. How easy it would
have been to stop. How much social media had primed me

to believe that a debut author could not possibly be a brown woman in her forties. How I might have never seen any of my books reach the readers that were looking for them if I had let what I'd thought was my expiration date take me off the damn shelf. Because here's the thing about expiration dates: They aren't real. They're made of whispers and insecurities and Instagram ads and someone else's idea of what is possible for you. But they're not made of you. (Your writing is made of you.)

Here is what I wish someone could have whispered to me back then: There is no expiration date on creation. There is no cutoff point for applying and reapplying yourself to the work you love. There is no list that will feel better than showing up for yourself and your pages, and every time you do it, you get closer to the readers who are looking for you. So keep going today. You're right on time.

THESE WORDS ARE FOR YOU AND ME

Did you know I say all these words to you as much as I say them to myself? That every day I get up in the morning and I have to tell myself to sit down and do the work? I've been writing books a long time, and it's the same challenge every day and it's a gift and a blessing that I'm allowed to do it, but it's always hard. And it's something worth fighting for. The writing.

4

SPRING

We all start our projects with enthusiasm and excitement, but do we always know how we're going to manage the work? Showing up feeling prepared and ready is the next big goal. Entering your projects with confidence is important. Approaching your work feeling like you can accomplish it rather than feeling like it's some insurmountable challenge. So how do we set ourselves up to feel that way? One way to start is by deciding on something small that can help lend a specific structure to our process. Like picking the spot where we sit and do the work.

I live in a small house—a little less than a thousand square feet—on a busy street in New Orleans. There are two front rooms, a long hallway with three rooms off to the side, and one back room. It's a classic shotgun house, designed that way to help promote air circulation in the summer.

If I sit in the front of the house, I can hear traffic going by starting in the morning straight through the early evening. I can also hear people talking as they pass by on the street, music coming from cars, and the squeaking sound of the bus stopping every half hour or so on the corner. None of it is particularly distracting, but, for the daylight hours, it is *constant*.

If I sit in the rear of the house, in my office facing onto the backyard, I can still hear the traffic, but it's muted, more like waves crashing. When the weather is nice, I sit with the back door open, and I can hear birds chirping, and sometimes a neighboring dog barks or an air-conditioning unit starts rumbling. But mostly it's pretty quiet.

In the front of the house, I sit at a long table made of cypress, and it faces a curtained window.

In the back of the house, I have a desk that was built for me, high enough so that I can look through the window at my garden and the dog. There I feel alone, and I can think, but every so often I catch myself feeling a little isolated. In the front of the house, I am aware that I'm not alone in the world, which is a comfort, a balm, but also I am perhaps too aware of the world to be fully immersed in my work.

My house provides me with everything I need to write, but at no point do I have all of it at once. But that's okay, because my needs are always changing anyway. I explore so many possible paths every day in my work. I'm always in the state of beginning, planning, thinking, except when I'm in the state of finishing, and even then—even then!—I could come up with something new: a newsletter idea, a distant idea for a new novel, a social media post that would make people laugh for two seconds—which isn't a bad day's work, to make someone laugh.

Every day what I need to be a creative and productive person shifts a little bit, either by my own making or because of external forces, but my desire to write remains the same. My focus, my end goal of making my art, stays true and steady. And I know I'll at least always be in the one place I need to be, which for me, at this moment in my life, is home.

Picking your spot is important. Knowing where you'll be every day to write can be a stabilizing force. It's a small gesture, yes, deciding where you'll write, but it's an important step in setting yourself up for success. And it can help you unfold a new sensibility about your relationship with your work. How important is it to you to concentrate your energy in a specific direction in service of your words? To organize your space, time, life, so that you can be productive? How much do you want to write?

Claim that spot. Claim it all.

LAURA VAN DEN BERG

For a long time, I never had a morning routine. Mornings were for caffeinating and feeding the dog; I didn't give them much thought. But last fall, my job expanded and though this was a welcome change in some ways, I could foresee what it meant for my writing time—or, more accurately, for the headspace I need to make any time I spend writing worthwhile. I needed to figure out how to open some new rooms in my brain and to keep those doors propped open, and since I am artistically useless after about four in the afternoon, I decided to reconsider my mornings.

I made a deal with myself: wake up an extra hour early and spend part of that time reading and the other part writing by hand. Other days, I would work more, but this morning routine is something I would do daily, no matter what. Mornings came to feel like a blueprint for the rest of the day, as I felt my imagination continuing to work on whatever I had written in that early quiet. I find that it's critical to stay in close contact with a project, so that I'm putting new words down and also so that the subconscious stays activated. This subtle shift in practice became a way to stay "in contact" even as there were intense demands on my time.

We are all different people with different responsibilities. Maybe you can only do thirty minutes or maybe you can listen to a recording of a story you love while you walk the dog. Maybe you are artistically useless in the morning and would benefit from being more intentional about your nights. Here is the bottom line: I think often of what a painter said to me at a residency: "Work makes more work." Indeed it does. Let's do what we can.

PICK A DATE

Pick a date in the distance and make a promise to accomplish something by that date. Your schedule gives your process a spine. You could even plot an entire timeline, a rough estimate of how long you think it will take you to finish each step of the way. Everyone's breakdown is different, of course. The first three chapters, the first one hundred pages, the first two parts of the book, the first draft, the second revision, and so forth. Don't be afraid to play around with these goals. But then hold yourself to them. Write to the future, write to those deadlines. There's something about breaking the big project into parts. So that it does not seem like an entire book but instead a series of goals. It's less intimidating. These smaller goals put things within reach.

KNOWING YOUR SKILLS

Recognizing where your talent lies is its own skill. Knowing what we need to work on in our craft is crucial. We all have blind spots. (I, for example, would happily shove all my characters in a room forever and make them talk and talk and never let them go anywhere unless someone gently reminds me to push them out the door.) But seeing what your strengths are, how to shine, how you can really dazzle, make your words glide and soar and move, that's just as important. We need to know how to succeed.

I want you to contemplate all the things you're best at in your work, the areas where you feel most confident and free, when you're having the best time, and there is an ease and flow to it all. Possibly you've gotten feedback in these areas before. Perhaps a reader or a teacher or a friend has noticed you're good at something. And that little pat on the head has meant a lot to you.

Make a list, if you like. Perhaps your strongest skill is writing dialogue, too. You just love to play around with witty banter. Maybe you're all about your characters, you're able to be loose and funny with them, you know what their habits are and how to dress them, and you just like spending time with them. Maybe you're good at sad, sweet moments. Maybe you write beautiful, long sentences. Or you're best at writing amazing sex scenes.

Now spend one day just leaning into that sweet spot. Let yourself fly and succeed and feel great about yourself and write the thing that satisfies a specific urge to be unquestionably your best. Don't hammer away, don't tinker, don't struggle for the moment. For just one day give yourself a little gift of easy success and see what comes out of it. See how it drives you through one day and then the next. Return to those skills when you need them. They don't run out, they don't disappear. They'll always be waiting.

CARMEN MARIA MACHADO

Writing is such a bizarre process. Sometimes I find it useful
to force myself to sit down and work, the old butt-in-chair
method that people love to talk about on panels and during
Q & As. But I think there is something to be said for the
vagaries of the human mind, its strange corridors and hidden
pockets, the firing of synapses across half a dozen associa-
tions before landing in a parallel universe your conscious
brain wasn't even aware existed. Your subconscious is your
best friend as a writer; it spits out beautiful, bizarre ideas
and solves narrative problems and also has a wicked sense
of humor. So many magical and memorable moments of
my own work emerged from that under-place. The girls-
with-bells-for-eyes from "Especially Heinous"? Came to me,
unbidden, in the shower, halfway through shampooing my
hair. And that process cannot be triggered by putting your
butt in a chair; it requires you to be flexible, thoughtful, and
purposeful about the way you collect, catalog, and access
your own ideas.

One of the most useful things I've ever read about process is an essay Kelly Link wrote about narrative obsessions
in 2010. I read it just before I entered grad school, and it

established in me a very healthy relationship with my brain; so much so that while I experience all kinds of impediments to my work that are outside my control (mental health, time, money), I have never experienced writer's block. Because I am constantly nursing my obsessions: reading about what excites and interests me, rejecting ideas of high- and lowbrow, letting myself indulge in narrative pleasures however and wherever they appear. And I'm constantly stumbling across ideas: riding the trolley, walking through my city, reading books, driving, cleaning. And the minute they come to me— no matter what I'm doing—I write them down. (If I have my phone, I record them in Evernote, but you don't need a special piece of software; you can jot it down in a notebook or on an old receipt, or text it to yourself, or leave yourself a voice note, as long as you remember to put it somewhere accessible later.)

And then when my butt is finally in that chair, I can look at the note I took four months ago—when I was not really in a place to write but the idea came to me just the same—and discover that I'm ready to make something of that little nugget from the past. Or that there are a bunch of nuggets over the course of a long period of time that string together into something interesting. Or that I've solved a long-standing narrative problem while vacuuming. Or whatever.

Which is to say: Feed your brain. Take care of it. Let it do things in its own way. Because if you can't trust your brain, what can you trust?

HOW TO WRITE WHEN
YOU HAVE A FULL-TIME JOB

I can't tell you how to organize your time exactly. There are little suggestions I have made to people along the way. Get up an hour earlier; write constantly, whenever you can. Take a notebook with you on the train, if you commute, or write during your lunch break. Keep a separate notebook next to you on your desk so you can scribble things down, and have it be just yours, even if it's only to serve as a reminder that your writer self exists no matter what.

When I wasn't yet a full-time writer, what worked for me was taking on freelance jobs for extended periods of time, saving my money, and then taking a month or so off and just working intensely on my writing. I wrote the first draft of my first novel during a summer off, but I worked in offices for the next eight years, and it was only with the publication of my fourth novel in 2012 that was I finally able to be a writer full-time. (And I had to pay a lot of debt off first!) It's extremely difficult to make a living solely as a writer. Practically every writer I know has teaching gigs or freelance writing gigs alongside their own practice.

What I want to suggest to you is that you look at your job and see what you can take from it, and I'm not just talking about office supplies but also, yes, I'm talking about office supplies.

I worked in advertising, writing bits of terrible copy to keep the lights on. Some things I learned in advertising ended up helping me as a novelist, but also in general as a creative person: how to write and produce quickly. How to receive and manage criticism—especially from people you've only just met. How to churn out a lot of ideas every day. That no idea was ever necessarily perfect. There was almost always a hole to be punched in it, so you had to find that hole before anyone else. And, perhaps most importantly, how to not feel precious about your work.

What things can you take from your job and apply to your writing? Is it about listening to the way people talk to each other? Are you learning the nitty-gritty specifics of something you could use for a character? Is there a mentor there who will encourage and support you creatively? Can you take a continuing education class that your employer will pay for? In this capitalist society, how can you bend it to your benefit?

J. COURTNEY SULLIVAN

If you are reading this—whether you've published ten books or two books or no books—you are a writer. Which means you are probably highly sensitive and possess the sort of intense empathy that might make it impossible to push the world away and get to work in dark times like these.

Don't push the world away. Be in it. The world needs people like you. There will be days to write gorgeous prose and days when it is enough just to keep your story alive. Maybe you write a thousand crappy words today, but they are the map that leads you to the good stuff.

For the first six months of my son's life, we had no childcare. I had in my head the idea for a novel about a new mother and the college-aged babysitter she hires. I couldn't manage to write actual scenes. But almost every day, and in the middle of the night, I sent myself emails from my phone with the subject line "Babysitter." They contained observations, ideas, bits of dialogue that arose for the book I had no time to write. After six months, when I started writing that book in earnest, the first thing I did was search my inbox for the word "Babysitter" and there they were—all the glorious breadcrumbs I'd left for myself.

This might be a breadcrumb moment for you. It is for me. I feel wrung out. Heartsick. I am glued to the news and Twitter. I saw a photograph online of George Floyd as a toddler in his mother's lap, and I can't get the image out of my mind.

My son is a month shy of three now. My daughter is eighteen months old. Thanks to COVID-19, my husband and I are in our thirteenth week without childcare. Our children say the words "I want" four thousand times a day. It is our job to fulfill these wants. Or deny them and face their toddler wrath. (As in our current stalemate over how many popsicles one small person should be allowed to eat before noon.)

Solitude is essential for many of us writers, and if we live with other people, it's precisely what our lives lack now. I wrote my first two novels while I had a full-time day job. I wrote them late at night. I still get my best work done between 11:00 p.m. and 2:00 a.m. I think most writers with other jobs and/or young children write while everyone else is asleep. There are those who work the early shift and those, like me, who stay up late. The only real writing I've done since March 13, 2020, has happened after midnight.

When you do sit down to write, whether you have an hour or all day, make a brief but meaningful transition in your body and your brain. Slow down. Hide your phone. Take three long deep breaths. Read poetry for a few minutes. Or spend a few minutes copying the style of Joe Brainard's gorgeous memoir, *I Remember*, in which the author starts every sentence with the two words in the title. See where that takes you.

A writer's time is precious. You know what none of us has the time for right now? Self-doubt. Two years ago this month, I was teaching a workshop, and my students and I made a pact. It would be the Summer of No Angst. Meaning we would waste no time doubting our talent, our originality, our work. We would not wonder if this thing we were writing might hurt someone's feelings or if it might be better to try and sound like that other writer, whom everyone seemed to adore. No. We would simply plow ahead. We would not try to become enlightened or to love every word we wrote, because we would surely fail on both counts. We just told ourselves we were putting off writerly negativity for a while. It worked. I'm doing it again now. Maybe you should, too. When doubt rises up, you tell it, "Nothing personal, but I think we should spend some time apart. See you in September."

AMANDA MULL

I'm a procrastinator. Not one who ruins her life with the habit, at least so far, but something in my psyche has a very difficult time starting work I don't want to do, which is any work. For years, I had a full-time job in the fashion industry while I tried to build a freelance writing career on nights and weekends, and it was an absolute slog: constant deadline anxiety, little sleep, beating myself up for not sitting down to write instead of just, you know, sitting down to write.

Despite the fact that I'm here to give advice, I haven't really solved that problem, but I have learned some more about myself, which is as close as you'll ever get to a solution to a lot of things. Most of my assignments are around two thousand words, and I have two or three days to report and write them, but no matter what I'm assigned, no matter how long it needs to be or when it's due, the biggest problem is the first three hundred words or so.

Writing, for me, is all about momentum. If I can write the first three hundred words, the next 1,700 are often like a boulder rolling down a hill once it's been pushed out of its comfortable divot at the top. I sometimes procrastinate on the three hundred words, too, but it's a much less daunting thing to ask of myself than to sit down and write a whole piece—it's a few grafs, half a page of a Google Doc, an amount of writing I might do without thinking when composing instructions for a new dog sitter. Their creation is what stands in my way, so now I do my best to just *write them*. Maybe I come back at the end and write a whole different lede instead, maybe my editor throws them out and wants something different up top, but just getting those words out, even if they're bad, is what unlocks all the other work for me. You have to figure out what your lock is, and its key.

HOW TO KEEP YOUR FINGERS IN IT

When I know it's necessary to take time away from my main creative project, usually because I have some other kind of work to do, I make sure to pay some attention to it regardless, to keep my fingers in it.

The most helpful strategy for me is to look at the work every day even if it's just for the briefest of time. To touch it, think about it, so it still feels fresh and luminous in my mind. I will just open up whatever I've been working on and reread it for five minutes, ten minutes, maybe write a little note to myself about it, even rework one sentence just for fun.

This does not feel like "writing" but it does feel like "doing work." It's so we can say to ourselves that we got a little bit done today as opposed to nothing at all. Nothing at all can sometimes feel fantastic, and our brains may need the break. I fully recommend nothing at all when you need it. But if you want to feel like you're still connected to your project and are trying to be an active participant in it even when time does not allow it, I suggest a daily, gentle acknowledgment of your work.

I also make sure to read. *If I don't have time to write, I sure don't have time to read*, you say to me. *I'm too busy.* You are not too busy to read a poem. You are not too busy to go to your bookshelf and pick up one of your favorite books and read the first few paragraphs of it. You are not too busy to engage intellectually with the work of others for a few stolen moments. Keep your brain limber and ready for the time when you can go back to your work and love it again.

And then when the time comes to resume your work, it will suck for a while, but it will suck less than if you hadn't done these things. And eventually the writing will feel just like you remembered, because that is how it works. It always affects your heart and brain in exactly the same way. Writing is magic, and writing is eternal. Don't you want to feel that way right now?

How To Gently Restart

—

- Remind yourself of what the project is and why you wanted to write it. Write it down. Just the sheer act of defining my project helps me to reclaim it for myself. Activate your imagination. It's not like flipping a switch, obviously; if it were that easy, we'd all be writing all the time. But the brain needs to be warmed up after disuse. It starts with remembering our whats and whys.
- Reread it all starting from the beginning. I know sometimes there's an unfamiliar feeling that can come with revisiting work that you haven't looked at in a while. This can feel sort of shocking and can even make you feel a little off-balance. After you read it, if it's possible, take a half-hour walk. Do not take your phone with you. Just walk. Let the words sit in your mind. Let them take up residence anew. It's time to let them take over your world again.
- Read the first chapter of a book you love to see how the author made it work, and then think about how it makes you feel.

- A little forgiveness, followed by a lot of focus. You don't have to be at your usual level of productivity the first day back. Cut yourself some slack if you only get your hands a little dirty at first. But I would shoot for returning to your usual word count in a few weeks' time. Don't let yourself off the hook. It's time to get back to work.
- Set yourself up for success physically and mentally. Make a plan for when you are going to dive back into it. Go to sleep early the night before, get up a little earlier. Tighten all those screws. Say to yourself, "The writing starts now."
- Ban yourself from the internet for the first few days. You can take the day off from "knowing things." There is nothing you will be missing all day that you can't learn about at the end of the day. You can ask a friend to text you if anything important happens if you absolutely *must know*. But just remember, it's time to reclaim your brain.
- Above all, do not feel intimidated or discouraged. You have written before, and you will write again. You write because you love it and because it's important to you and because you have something to say. Don't see it as an insurmountable challenge but rather as an opportunity to grow.

REBECCA CARROLL

I write at the kitchen table, which is at the center of our apartment. It's attached to the living room, where the TV is, and the apartment is small to begin with. I write when my teenage son is watching TV, and though he watches most of his shows and movies on his phone, the quarantine has made him yearn for a change of venue every so often. But even before the pandemic, I wrote an entire book during both the NFL and NBA 2019 seasons—my son and husband are rabid fans.

I take breaks to make my son breakfast and lunch, and then sit back down to write. I answer his questions and try to mitigate his boredom now that we're in lockdown all day while simultaneously working. Since he can't get to the barber, he recently decided that rather than risk trusting me to give him a proper line-up, he's giving over to growing his hair out. Every few days, he sits on the floor between my legs and I twist his hair into drop twists while we watch an episode of *Riverdale*.

I guess I've always written and created within a certain measure of chaos—emotional, psychological, logistical. My overall approach in everything I do is and has always been collagist. I find inspiration in the elegant clutter of things. The art on our walls, the books on our shelves, the sound of trap music that spills from my son's headphones. My writing is in conversation with the tenor of our lives.

ADA LIMÓN

I think one of the things that helps me write is, simply, silence. It's boring, I know. But we are never quiet anymore. When was the last time you went for a walk and didn't listen to music or a podcast or a book or decide to call your mother. Silence is where the writing comes from, that voice underneath the voice that we try our best to tamp down and gag with distractions and anxiety-inducing self-loathing. If we are really listening, though, the world opens up in a way that it doesn't to everyone all the time. It opens as a way of being generous to us, a reward for listening. We have to be tender to the world, we have to make ourselves tender to the world. We must be the receiver before we can be the maker. It doesn't have to be meditation (but it helps!) or long walks on the beach. It can just be a small errand you choose to do in silence: laundry, a drive to the pharmacy, weeding. If you can allow yourself that space, a shift will happen; underneath the buzz of the world, there's a story starting, a poem begin-ning, a deep noticing that at once feels surreal and more real than anything else. That's where the writing begins.

I've mentioned I never got an MFA. That meant I had to build a writing cohort from scratch. I didn't have an instant peer group. People I trusted, or people who trusted me. Or who liked my work. I was disconnected, at first.

I have absolutely no statistics to back this up (although I bet someone does), but I feel certain there are just as many—if not more—writers getting published who don't have an MFA as those who do. That doesn't mean it's not hard to form a writing community. But just to say, there's a lot of us working and thriving without an advanced degree.

The most helpful action I took early in my writing life, hands down, was going to readings, and then, later, forcing myself to do open mics at readings. I met so many people that way, and even if we didn't sustain relationships forever, it's that kind of churn of new ideas and personalities that can help mutually drive writing.

I'm always excited to meet other writers. There is just this exquisite sense of finding my people. We are the same kind of awkward. All those readings I went to, all those drinks after literary conferences, all those emails I sent, all those tweets I liked. I did it because I meant it. The extra gift is that these people end up being your best cheerleaders and critics alike. I found the ones who would tell me the truth and who wanted me to succeed—and I have tried to be that person for them, as well.

Of course, this was in NYC in the early aughts, a very specific scene, a very specific time. But I think the logic behind it still applies: finding people who are at the same place as you in your career, with the same level of energy, too.

There are non-MFA programs that offer writing workshops. These programs can be about not only improving your writing but also tuning up your brain and connecting with other writers. You may find an accountability partner in the class or even be able to eventually turn the workshop into a separate writers' group after the class ends.

You can also post a notice at cafés or libraries to see if anyone is looking to start a writers' group online or in person. Having a regular set time to discuss your (and their) writing with people is a great first step to building a community.

And of course, there is the internet, which works best when things happen organically or accidentally. This is how I've made some of my best writing friends. By liking things someone else says or likes, by paying attention to what people say, and not just skimming. Looking for depth, stumbling on ideas. Craving collaboration, a shared sense of something bigger than myself, and finding people seeking the same. If this is starting to sound less like advice and more like a personal ad for friendship, it probably is.

Because I understand your feelings deeply. I have always wanted a writing community myself. I would hurl myself at a writer I liked when I was first starting out—and I still do. The beauty is there are so many kinds of writing communities out there, because there isn't just one kind of writer. Even with my own sphere, I have different kinds of friendships, and I bet lots of people reading this do, too.

Some things to consider: Are you trying to write the same kind of form or genre? Do you have the same taste in books? Is it just that you live in the same city? Do you all have children and are just trying to steal time to write? Is your writing pace compatible, or are you competitive in a friendly way and drive each other to finish your work? Do you just like to make fun of other writers? Is your writing time just a gossip session to let off steam? Is it a way for you to walk and talk and get some fresh air? Or can you sit alone in a room (or online) together in utter silence and scribble furiously in your notebook, feeding off each other's energy? Followed by one stiff drink, perhaps. Cheers, we survived another week.

I don't consider myself a friendly person, and yet, I am a maker of friends. Because I appreciate them so damn much. We need each other in this lonely profession. You can't force a relationship, but you still have to make some effort. Take a class, join an online discussion, reach out as much as you can. There's someone like you waiting on the other end. Trying to connect.

R. O. KWON

For the first couple of months of the pandemic, I wrote one line of my novel a day. I could barely read, let alone write, but I still had this thin line to my life's work. It was all I could do; it wasn't enough.

Then, last May, I started an accountability group with several dear writer friends, then added a second group with a couple of other close friends, so that now, usually every day, I tell these two groups what I've written that day, and they tell me. I try to write a certain number of words a day, while some friends are measuring the day by how long they wrote, and so on. What I realized is that while I tend to try hard to live up to my promises to others, I am equally good at breaking promises to myself—I mean, it's just me, here I am, why not. It's helped so very much to tie each day's writing to the first tendency, not the second. And what a joy it is that, physically separated though we mostly still are, I daily have these friends at my side.

CYNTHIA D'APRIX SWEENEY

Writing is a solitary business, and those of us who spend our days trying to conjure an imaginary world have to do whatever we can to engage in the real one. If hopping onto social media alleviates your loneliness and brings you pleasure, I'm not going to clothe it in shame. *However,* I would urge you to pay attention to how your trusty diversions make you feel and whether they nourish or deplete your creative soul. When my writing day begins, I fire up an app called SelfControl (purchased because I have none) to block social media and a handful of other sites for six or seven hours. That I am easily distracted is one reason, but the more relevant reason is that I'm a better writer when I shut out a certain type of noise for at least a few hours. When I'm writing, I think of my heart and my brain as being tethered by a vital, slender thread that I have to protect. I'm very picky about the voices I let into my head. I'm not advocating getting off Facebook as much as I am gently suggesting that you identify the ways you might be avoiding—as the late great David Rakoff put it—the deeply unglamorous task of tolerating yourself long enough to push something out.

I BET THIS IS YOUR BIGGEST DISTRACTION

I used to smoke cigarettes, for a long time, maybe twenty years. Somewhere in that time, I read an interview with a British writer—I can't remember who it was now—where he talked about smoking cigarettes, even as an older man who should probably have known better by then, but he just couldn't stop. He said that when he was smoking he always felt like he had twenty best friends in his pocket. That made so much sense to me. There was always something to do when cigarettes were around. There was always a good time to be had, even if it would only last for a minute or two. You were never really alone if you had cigarettes.

I think about this a lot now when I think about my relationship with my phone. The fact that I can always reach one of my actual living best friends when I have my phone in my pocket, which is perhaps why I carry it with me so much or fall asleep with it resting on my bedside table. And does it make me feel a little safer to know it's there? Perhaps.

But also, I know that when I reach for it first thing in the morning instead of a notebook or a book to read, I'm making a specific choice not to engage with my brain creatively. I'm looking for friends, or information, but not inspiration. Often, I'm giving into the lazier part of my brain that doesn't quite want to start working yet in the way that creativity demands. Sometimes I get distracted by my phone for twenty minutes, forty minutes, an hour, and I look up and those minutes are gone, and I could have been reading a book that entire time.

My main sticking point is when I take walks. I like to listen to music on my walk, or sometimes I call my parents or friends. I like to take pictures of street cats in my neighborhood or flowers growing up from the sidewalk, and I find it comforting to share these images on the internet. How can that be bad?

But on the other hand, what about if I walk without a computer in my pocket and see things and clear my head and contemplate the world without a lens? What about that?

All right, what about the fact that I'm writing this now by typing it into an email to myself? It's made my life as a writer easier, or at least easier for certain kinds of writing, although I'm not sure if I'm doing necessarily *better* writing. It's just so quick to type it in this manner. A thousand words can blow by so quickly.

But am I missing out on a possibly better albeit slower kind of writing because I'm just using this tiny screen which forces me, in a way, to think in a tiny box?

I did come up with the idea to write about this topic when I was scribbling in my journal. I went to my favorite local wine shop, and I bought a glass of wine, and I sat with my journal and was alone in my own thoughts, away from screens. It's actually good not to have my best friends (or a simulation of them) near me at all times. It's actually healthy to be alone. And for me it's so important to write things down in a notebook because I can never lie to myself when I'm writing by hand. My hand will not form dishonest words, whereas when I text or type into my phone, the possibilities of alterations, shading, filtering, are extremely present. And even when I'm writing fiction, I still need to be telling the truth.

Before the pandemic I was better at separating my life from my phone. But then there was a long stretch where it felt crucial to have it on me at all times. What if I missed some news? And the idea of being alone was fraught in a new way. I needed to feel connected. It was just so easy to slip into it all feeling necessary.

But I'm getting much, much better at separating myself from it again. I know how to leave it in the other room if I want to concentrate on my work. I know how to take a walk without it and just put a notebook in my pocket if I think I'll have some ideas I want to capture. I know how to turn it off, put it away—I just don't do it all the time, or as much as I'd like. But I'm getting there.

I think about how I quit smoking, too, even though it's been ten years already. I like to tell the story where I quit smoking in an instant. I was meditating and a voice came into my head that said that I needed to stop punishing myself with smoking and then I never desired another cigarette again. This is one truth. But the other truth is that I quit and started again for a number of years, so in a way I was quitting the whole time, and that was just the moment where it finally worked. Still, I recognize the importance of that one moment where I said to myself: Stop punishing yourself.

How does technology play into your work? Are you punishing or rewarding yourself with it? Does it impact your work positively or negatively? Is it possible to cut down on your usage of it? I ask you these questions because I'm always asking myself these questions. I don't have all the answers, but at least I know I need to find them.

ELISSA WASHUTA

I never closely tracked my writing process until people began asking me how I wrote the book they just read. I have no idea how that happened. A mystical process, or one I just never paid attention to, because all my attention was on the essay rather than its making.

So lately, I've been keeping track of how it's going. I didn't intend to make myself start writing a new book until I was done promoting my last one, but then I *wanted* to write. Here's how it's been going: first, I took interest in something, and I got wrapped up in it, because it was a situation with an unfolding narrative I found compelling. I found myself spending a good amount of my free time learning about this thing, and then compulsively bookmarking things I read online, and then, one day when I was hauling canned cat food up from the basement, a sentence implanted itself in my brain. The sentence wouldn't leave, and then it spawned another, and then I had to capture them in a Word document so I wouldn't forget them.

I resisted the paragraph—the timing was bad. I couldn't start a new essay. I need long, long stretches of hyperfocus in order to make an essay. I need to hand over whole days. But I couldn't risk losing the sentences because they'd become precious to me. So I wrote my paragraph. For two months, all I had was that paragraph and its fully realized voice, an uncountable number of bookmarks, and my fear that I took too long to write the thing and now the window was closed. I kept thinking over the question of what the following paragraphs would be—a question that I didn't feel I could really answer without having some sense of the essay's form. It won't come if I try writing to see what comes out. There will be words I can use later, but the form doesn't come that way for me. I can't make an outline. My brain just has to draw up the blueprints while I'm thinking about something else.

About a week ago, overwhelmed by the fact of being reachable by anyone in the world at any time, I decided to mostly stop using social media for a little while. While I was trying to learn how to fly a video game airplane, my mind was listlessly wandering back and forth over the not-yet-existent essay, not actively problem-solving but just thinking about some minutiae of the subject matter, and then, suddenly, there was the form of the essay. I wrote down some notes, and then the next day, when I was supposed to be working on something else, I wrote more notes, and then I couldn't stop writing notes, and then there was the shape of the essay, an almost three-dimensional holographic thing in my imagination. Next I will have to begin to write into the form, and I'll soon begin failing, and I'll wonder whether I can even execute this vision I had, and in the end, the real essay will and will not look like the hologram I imagined—it always turns out better. I have to remember that so I can start again.

THE SUPPLIES

What objects will inspire you either intellectually or emotionally? Do you need to buy a new notebook? Do you need to treat yourself to a cool pen? (God, I love a cool pen.) Do you want to ask a peer or a local bookseller for recommendations for something that would be helpful to read for inspiration? Do you need a box of a specific tea to drink that you associate with some of your most productive moments? Once my friend Karolina Waclawiak sent me a crystal, which sounds pretty hippie-dippie, but just the idea that this specific object was meant to inspire me alone was enough to warm up my brain.

Make sure you have all your shit together, in one place, so nothing can slow you down once you start to write.

ALEXANDER CHEE

I was in Denver and about to begin teaching. It was Pride that day, and the Office Depot I was at was right at the center of the parade. I needed a phone cord, my one errand, and yet there I was, in the stationery aisle.

I don't lack for projects presently—a new novel underway, another one also, a new collection of essays almost done. I have different paper notebooks for each project, in a stack in my office.

And what I know by now: the legal pad and pen is like a change in the wind in my heart, the new idea raising its hand. The notebook makes room for it, and the pen is the door it opens to walk out. A tiny door the size of where the ink comes out. And it cost me less than ten bucks for the pens and the notebook.

When I'm starting something new, I back into it, trick myself into writing by acting like I'm just interested in a place, an event, a person out of history or who has left some mark on my imagination. A couple I met on a train or a guy driving around on a bicycle with his dogs in a cart on the back, blasting NKOTB's "You Got It (The Right Stuff)" out of an amp. I turn it into a question. Answering the question, "Who is Jenny Lind?" was how I found *The Queen of the Night*.

Something I hear from my students over and over again is how they don't know how to make space in their life for the writing. I get it. But this is one way to make space if, say, you can't grow a room to put your desk in. Yes, time matters. Energy matters. Space. Don't make it too precious but don't overlook the simple answers. A laptop can feel like a smeary stage with too much light for a rehearsal, much less a warm-up. Paper notebooks won't. They have no notifications except this one, telling you to go write. A place you can play in alone with the story that has started to tell itself to you in your mind.

This may not be your process, but . . . take some time and identify yours. Learn to hear when the idea wants you to at least look sideways. And have a place where it can happen.

LOOK UP

If I could, I would buy you all a plane ticket to anywhere in the world you want to go. I want a delicious meal in an unexpected corner of the world for all of you. Or the chance to reunite with an old friend you haven't seen in a million years. Or the chance to be by yourself, quiet in your head, witnessing something brand new. I want travel and growth and opportunity for all of you.

Travel has always been important for me. Just hitting the road in whatever way was accessible, driving cross-country, trains to different cities, even just to see a new place for the day. When I was younger and still lived in New York, I rode my bike all over the city in search of a new café or a sculpture garden I hadn't seen before. Or I just walked everywhere I could, eyes up, paying attention, watching, listening. Whenever I travel now and I find that I'm gazing at my phone for too long, I whisper to myself, "Look up." That's my trick. That's my phrase to relieve myself from being sucked into a screen, to be out in the world more. I'm always reminding myself to do that. Be curious about everything, I tell myself. Look up.

STRENGTH-TRAINING

—

You will write these 1000 words because it can help you build strength—artistically, intellectually, professionally, and emotionally. You're doing real labor here: creating a space for yourself out of thin air, each word on top of another. Stairs to the sky, a bridge to a fantastic location. It's heavy lifting, writing these words every day, but you will see real results. Close your eyes, picture the physicality of what you're doing. You're building a future with your words.

MAGGIE SHIPSTEAD

Sometimes, especially in a first draft, I get paralyzed by a fear of doing it wrong, of taking an approach that I'll eventually have to undo. I might be worried about a question of plot, or I might be unsure about the voice I've adopted, obsessing over first person versus third or present tense versus past. It's difficult for me to make peace in advance with the inevitable detours, backtracks, wrong turns, dead ends, flat tires. Other times I forge ahead while a big red light flashes that what I'm doing isn't working. I'm ever hopeful that the flashing light is wrong, that, down the road, my first readers will reassuringly contradict the warning. This has never happened.

My gut instinct that something isn't working has always been correct, but—maybe paradoxically—my instinct to push through anyway has also been correct. I needed to put down the wrong thing in order to be able to let it go. The inherent inefficiency of writing fiction makes me anxious, but I think being anxious is a necessary, if unpleasant, part of my process. Writing is really hard, and making peace with it being hard is hard, too. Sometimes you're gonna do it right, and sometimes you're gonna do it wrong. The stuff you get right on the first try won't necessarily be better than the stuff you have to grind away at forever. Probably none of it will ever be perfect because nothing is. So cut yourself some slack. Accept the mess.

I think about this all the time, how nothing is ever perfect. How the biggest trick we can play on ourselves is thinking we can make our work, art, life exactly correct. How we can tread water forever if we get mired in that headspace. Just get the words down on the page today, and then fix them later. You know how to do this. Just write.

ON READING

Reading stimulates growth, both as a person and an artist. I read constantly, read everything, outside of my genre, too. So much poetry I have read. So much translated work I still need to read. Novels, short story collections, comics, books, magazines, plays, screenplays. It's all about storytelling, studying the structure, form, exposing yourself to new voices that inspire you. But also it's that reading is good for all artists, good for all people. We need to know the positive and negative alike in humanity. Reading is the surest path to understanding. It leads to a fullness within us.

ROLE MODELS

I have always looked for role models, especially when I was starting out, when everything felt so vast and wide and open to possibility—but dizzyingly so. How did these older writers know what to do? How did they know how to be? How did they figure it all out?

I read the collected diaries of writers. And I read interviews and personal essays and watched documentaries; I sat in the front row of readings and paid attention during the question-and-answer sessions. I was so grateful to every writer who was kind to me at a party I somehow got invited to (or crashed), or who offered the smallest amount of advice or encouragement, or bought me a drink, or gave me a cigarette. Or who led the way by being inventive in form or genre, or giving voice to characters of all kinds, or who smashed through glass ceilings or tore down the gates, leaving an open space for others to follow. I paid attention to them and was inspired by them. When I knew nothing, they were the ones I learned from.

Reading *The Diaries of Dawn Powell: 1931–1965* was a real breakthrough moment for me. Following her ups and downs over three decades, not only the struggles of being a writer but also the joys of the actual writing, the pleasure of its company. It made me feel less alone even as I knew how hard I would have to work . . . forever. And I always think about a particularly inspiring evening in Brooklyn watching Kelly Link and Benjamin Percy in conversation about world-building. So many things shifted in my brain at once that night. And I even remember Jonathan Lethem loaning me a cigarette outside a bar off Union Square after he had given a reading with David Sedaris and Heidi Julavits. I was in my twenties, broke, wide-eyed, just aspiring to be anything at all, and he was genuine and nice and generous, and I thought, *Oh, that's how you're supposed to be when you grow up.* (Minus the smoking part! Don't smoke, kids!)

Words on the page: the most important thing. But having an understanding of those who came before you, the work they've done, are still doing, can only help make the path in front of you a little brighter.

DEESHA PHILYAW

A few years ago, I interviewed Carmen Maria Machado for
Visible: Women Writers of Color, a monthly column I wrote at
the *Rumpus* at the time. I don't remember the exact question,
but something I asked prompted Carmen to liken her writing
process to solving a math problem. And when she said that,
my inner math geek rejoiced. Finally, I had words to describe
my approach to writing, a process driven by my curiosity,
quirks, and interests. Because when it comes to writing short
stories, I'm not an outliner; I'm a discoverer, a problem solver.

My love of math actually precedes my love of writing,
which didn't emerge until my late twenties. As a high school
senior, while everyone else complained about the fat packet
of four hundred calculus problems Ms. Madison assigned
us to complete *over spring break*,[1] I was secretly delighted.
There was, and still is, something very satisfying to me about
filling in blanks and finding solutions.

I write to figure out who my characters are—what they
want, where they've been, where they're going, who their

---

1 Thanks in part to Ms. Madison's relentlessness, I got a 5, the highest score
possible, on the AP Calc exam that year. Practice pays off, but that's a different essay for a different day.

people are, what terrifies them, what pleases them. I write to figure out how I can make their lives, or a moment in their lives, as complicated, messy, surprising, and compelling as possible. I write to uncover opportunities to subvert norms, upend expectations (including my own), say the unsayable, and trounce on tired tropes.

With these aims in mind, writing for me is sometimes a series of *if . . . then*, or conditional, statements, as in geometry: *If* my main character establishes firm, detailed rules of engagement in her affairs with married Christian men, *then* she'll maintain the upper hand in those relationships. And *if* she maintains control, *then* she will be happy. (This second conditional statement may be false; I'll leave it to the reader's interpretation.)

Other times, I'll take a guess-and-check approach, as in algebra. *Guess*: My main character ends up falling in love with one of the married men she sleeps with. *Check*: BORING. Been done a million times. So, I keep guessing and checking as to what happens with this character until my first reader (me) is satisfied.

Another algebraic approach involves solving for x, where
$$y = x + 2 \text{ of my characters who live on oppo-}$$
site coasts meet at a conference;
$$y = \text{they make love 9 months later.}$$
And x represents the obstacles I throw in this
couple's path before they get naked.

Sometimes, I solve for *why*. Given a discrete set of circumstances, vendettas, injustices, intergenerational traumas, and unfortunate events, why does my character do what she does? And how might the story's stakes change if she does the inverse of what she's always done or is expected to do?

As I said, my inner math geek lives for this kind of carrying on. Thinking of writing, particularly drafting, in this way invites a spirit of playfulness, possibility, and wonder into my writing practice, instead of fear, self-doubt, and worry. It's this spirit that brings me back to the page time and time again. And it's this spirit that allows me to welcome, rather than dread, narrative problems.

But maybe math isn't your thing. That's fine. The point is, it's okay not to know 100 percent what we're doing when we're writing. In fact, this mystery—of what our ramblings and meanderings might become—is more than okay, it's *good*. In a craft essay in *Brevity* magazine titled "Against the Shitty First Draft," Gabriela Denise Frank challenges the ubiquitous Anne Lamott dictum originally intended to guard against perfectionism in writing. She writes, "It's not a binary: writing doesn't have to be perfect on the first try or it's garbage. Art-making is a durational practice. We work the material, and the material works us."

Unlike artists in other disciplines, Frank notes, writers "can't purchase our first drafts from catalogs or quarries . . . [We] must conjure our medium and our tools. The first draft is our clay, our canvas, our film, and through revision we add shape, color, and focus. Have you ever heard a sculptor degrade the material she's chiseling a statue from? *Look at this shitty marble!*"

When I sit down to start a story or tackle a narrative problem, the block of marble feels like a nice, nerdy packet of four hundred calculus problems. Challenging, satisfying, doable. Working through each problem, I chip away at everything that isn't the story I'm trying to tell.

What does the marble feel like in your hands?

ON SAFETY

Writers need to feel safe in order to write. But that's not always available from the external world. Because of one's race, or because of one's gender, or because of one's domestic life, or because of the state of one's particular union, or because sometimes the world just feels like a very dangerous place—those are just a few examples—it can be hard to maintain a sense of safety or security.

It's not necessary to write from a place of love or peace. Often enough people write because they feel angry or scared or threatened or fired up, and all of those feelings are okay as inspirations or starting points. But still I want everyone to have a quiet room where they don't have to look over their shoulder, where they can shut out all the noise. A library carrel, an office after hours, an empty kitchen when no one's home from school or work yet.

If we're lucky enough to already have a secure feeling, can we look out for others around us who might not? How can we extend or share safety with others in our writing community?

Sometimes that quiet room simply has to be generated in our mind's eye. What I want is for everyone to feel secure enough to tell the truth. That your ideas are safe with you. You can do this by telling yourself you have a right to express what you have to say. Don't listen to anyone else but yourself. You deserve to tell your story. Give yourself that gift of safety. You are the one to make this decision for yourself and no one else.

WHAT I WANT YOU TO CARRY WITH YOU INTO YOUR WORK EVERY DAY AS IF YOU WERE A SOLDIER (AND I AM ARMING YOU FOR BATTLE)

Not every day of writing is going to feel successful. In fact, more than a few days may test your spirits because the words didn't flow effortlessly. Or there were too many distractions (not of your own making, obviously, for you would *never*) to get any kind of real rhythm going. Or maybe you just didn't have all the answers right away. Or maybe you had too many answers when you were looking for just one.

And to all that I say, you showed up, you did the work just by showing up and sitting there, and it will all pay off someday if you keep showing up. You can sit there feeling bad, with negativity soaring all around you, but I instead offer you this as a shield: it's just one bad day of writing, and they will not all be like that.

It's simply a fact that our creativity is uneven from day to day. There are days when I find myself just staring into space. Sometimes I get stuck on the same sentence for an hour (or two) straight. Or I rewrite a scene from scratch, but it still doesn't feel right. And I think: *What are these things called words? Do I even know how to write?*

But I have learned something important. The unsuccessful day of writing isn't a reflection of the quality of your brain or your commitment to your art. It is really, truly, just one bad day.

Don't let it throw you off. Do not lose faith in yourself. Do not lose heart.

Just start again tomorrow.

JASMINE GUILLORY

When I was in the middle of the draft for my third book, everything about it was harder than anything I'd written before. It was moving slower, it was taking me longer to figure out the characters, and the voice in my head telling me no one would like it was louder and louder. But all I could do was write my way through it. In my writing journal one day for that draft, I wrote, "Spent hours and hours today having a meltdown about this book, but then just made myself fucking work on it and I got a lot done." I spent the next few months just making myself fucking work on it (whether I had a meltdown or not).

There are a lot of things that go along with writing for me: anxiety; stress; uncertainty; confusion. There are also hope and joy and wonder and celebration, too, but the other things can sometimes drown the good parts out. But I've realized there's so much of this writing life I can't control—if people like my book, if people review my book well (or at all), if people buy my book, if people understand my book, the list goes on. But the one thing I can control is the work. I can make myself sit down and do the work, 1000 words at a time. And I've realized my goal in doing this work is to write a book that I love, and one that I'm proud of, and I control that, too. Realizing all of that pushed me to finish the draft of that book, and after five or six (or maybe more, I lose count) drafts, that book finally came out. I hoped other people liked it—don't get me wrong—but I was satisfied that I liked it first.

I have realized, as I keep on with this writing life, that every book is different, and often tips and tricks that work with one book don't work with the next one. But—and I have to remind myself of this anew with each book—the one thing that works, every single time, is just writing. Even when it's a bad writing day, even when I have to force myself to do it, I always feel better after I write.

GO WRITE ALREADY

You will stop pretending that the distraction is more powerful than your mind or your intentions. You are stronger than that, and you are hungrier than that. Recognize that your desires to write and be productive are more relevant to your happiness than whatever insignificant diversion you claim is preventing you from doing your work. Fuck your distractions. Go write already.

5

SUMMER

A friend of mine recently quit their job to try a different path—a thing I have done before, more than a few times. They were nervous but exhilarated about their choice. I told them about how there is always a down cycle before there is an up cycle. That whenever we make big shifts in our lives, it takes a while (don't ask me how long a while is; you'll know when it's over) to settle into this new rhythm. It's helpful to know why we've made the shift, although I recommend it being more than "just because." It's important to recognize that we'll be in transition for a while, and we must accept the struggles that come with that. This is an unsteady feeling, and that's why it's a risk. We could lose everything. What's harder in the moment is the *feeling* that we could lose everything. But of course, this makes us feel alive, too.

One year I wrote about thirty thousand words of a new book. The next year I realized that I had to stop where I was at that moment and write a new beginning for the book. Everything I had written was *fine*, just fine. I'm a perfectly competent sentence writer every day of the week, so what was on the page was adequate. And I had momentum. I knew where I wanted the story to go. I was afraid to take a break from that momentum—what if I didn't get it back? But my gut told me that I needed to walk back to the beginning of the story and take a look at the future as it spread out from there. Look at the source of the pain, I thought, and track the way it radiates. Then you can find your way to the end.

Anytime we shift directions in our writing, it feels tricky. Anytime we cut gigantic blocks of text, it seems like we could be making the biggest mistakes of our lives. Anytime we realize there should be a different protagonist from the one we began with in the first place? That is an "oh shit what if this doesn't work" state of mind. Anytime we take on material or structure or a form or a genre that's new from what we've worked with in the past, it feels like a huge fucking risk.

A friend of mine wrote a novel in first person, then revised and made the entire book close third with multiple perspectives, then went back *again* and revised it all in first person. An incredible risk each time. She spent so much energy. The risk of expending energy. What if we run out of it? (But we won't.) It must have felt terrifying.

Do we worry we're messing up our books/careers/lives each time we do this kind of thing? Yes. It's both an answer and a crisis to take these kinds of leaps with our work.

Anytime we write about a topic that makes us feel nervous, it's hard. Anytime we write from a place deep inside us that feels revolutionary. Anytime we write about something that feels intimate and personal. Anytime we write about something we think our parents wouldn't approve of. Or our friends. Or our lovers. Or potential employers. Or people with power. Anytime we write about something that feels new or different or radical or lays our heart on a plate for any old stranger to feast upon.

Anytime we say to ourselves: You know what? I'm going to spend the next few years of my life trying to write a book, and I may never get that time back, but if I don't try it, I'll never know if I could do it or not.

But now it's time to try.

TODAY YOU WILL WRITE 1000 WORDS

You will sit down at your desk or kitchen table or couch or at the café or the bar or the library or the break room or the park bench or the front seat of your car or wherever it is you go to write, and you will pull out your notebook or legal pad or phone or laptop or whatever it is you write on, and you will crank up some music or put in some earplugs or switch on an application that will block your internet access or whatever it is you need to do to shut out the noise, and you will sit up straight and you will turn your gaze inward and your imagination outward, and you will be disciplined and you will be rigorous and you will be determined, and you will write. One thousand words. Today.

KRISTEN ARNETT

Here's what I know:

I love garbage.

By that I mean I consider myself a connoisseur of everything trash. I love really cheap, shitty beer. I like making "chip salad" for dinner, which is essentially just mixing every kind of chip in the house into a mixing bowl and then calling it a salad so it will feel like I've had some kind of vegetable/nutrient. I occasionally forget to brush my hair. I have been known to kiss my dog directly on her dirty little head (please forgive me for this one, she's wonderful). It's just who I am.

But I am also a writer. And who I am as a person—the ways I choose to move through the world, dirty or clean—always comes directly into focus when I think about craft.

I am not a clean writer. I have very messy drafts. I do not outline. It's a form of chaos that makes sense to my rumpled, wrinkled brain. Occasionally, I will see how other people work and get an itch to neaten up a bit. To try and make sense of the scribbles I've jotted down on grease-soaked paper. To get more organized. To neaten my pages and subsequently my writer's mind.

This never works out well.

I find myself scrambling in an unfamiliar environment. I feel itchy and uncomfortable, trussed and confined, like trying to put on jeans that somehow got put into the wash. It doesn't fit me. It isn't easy or relaxed. I'm trying so hard to be neat that my creative side isn't allowed to run wild. Part of that comes from the need, I think, to be organized in ways that will make it so we won't fail. There is a very real fear of failure when it comes to writing, especially if it's work we want to show to others. We want to ready ourselves for success. To present the neat, clean work that shows we're competent and capable. But quite often, it's the messiest work that holds all the fun. The garbage is a hell of a good time.

So, dive into the dumpster. Wallow a little with your work. Let it eat a big bowl of leftover spaghetti out of a discolored Tupperware and then drop some of it down the front of its clean white opening page. There is so much good that can come from reveling in the mess. And hey, you can always worry about cleaning up later.

Let's get messy.

ATTICA LOCKE

My greatest piece of advice for writing is to approach the experience as play. Have fun. This is only possible if you write without judgment, and if you have tremendous compassion for yourself during the process. I live by the words of Jane Smiley in *Thirteen Ways of Looking at the Novel*: the only way you can fail at a first draft is by not finishing it. Sometimes when I'm not sure I have the bandwidth or energy to write but I know I need to, I tell myself this: just hang out with the work for an hour or so and see what happens. No judgment. It's the number one killer of creativity and productivity.

YOU ARE A PERSON WHO WRITES

You are a person who writes, whatever that might possibly look like for you. Maybe it means being a published author, maybe it means being a good communicator. Maybe you have stacks of filled journals all over your home which you look at fondly to remind yourself of all the thoughts you've had, all that you feel inside of you. (I do, anyway.) But you are a person who writes, you get to say that about yourself every day that you do it. Here is a thing I do, here is an important part of me: I write.

MEGAN ABBOTT

Write badly. Give yourself permission to write badly. Say to yourself, "I'm going to write the worst 1000 words ever put to paper."

Write crazy stuff. Give yourself permission to write crazy stuff. Say to yourself, "I'm going to write the craziest 1000 words ever put to paper."

Write before you're really awake. Give yourself permission to write when you're in that bleary dawn fog when your dreams are still mingling with your waking life. Say to yourself, "I'm going to write from that dim place in my head that I still have access to when I just wake up."

Say to yourself, "Before even coffee."

MIN JIN LEE

When I write, I allow myself the same heart I have when I read something fine and beautiful. I want to have a heart full of admiration and gratitude even for my very early drafts. I am not interested in noticing the things that don't or won't work when I am writing; all the editing and revisions will sort themselves out eventually. When I am writing and rewriting, I give myself freedom and permission to frolic in my infinite possibilities. I don't care if that sounds irrational, delusional, or foolish, because already, I am those things. I am a fiction writer, and being one means I don't expect to make sense to most upright folks. As a writer, of course, it is my job to write something worth sharing, but well before I can share, I must write and believe that I can. I am rooting for you, fellow writer. With all my heart.

LAUREN GROFF

What I would like for you to remember today is that your
work is a living thing. It exists outside of you; it has hungers
and fears and joys and lusts of its own. In some ways, this
can be a great comfort because your job is merely the job of
all the caretakers of wild beasts: you have to keep the work
fed, give it shelter and a place to exercise, allow it to nap and
roar and squeal and lunge and hide in the shade on a hot
day. On the other hand, taking care of anything and keeping
it alive is a responsibility that is not for the languid or the
halfhearted or the uncommitted. You have to wake up every
day ready to trot off and feed the beast.

What makes this all the more complicated is that you
will never quite know the mood of your work until you
visit it. Sometimes you get lucky and your work stalks you
like a tiger, and all you have to do is stand there and let it
leap on you. Most of the time, though, the work is shy. It is
more of a mouse or lemur than a tiger; it can often seem like
a drunken mistake on the part of the creator (you), something like a platypus or axolotl or blobfish. When your work
appears to you as small and furtive, you will have to show
up day after day, in silence and patience and hope, and try

your best, and a lot of the time it will only reveal a twitching nose or a fin before fleeing from your hand. You'll be left with a bunch of words that you know you'll destroy the next day. Or, you will be left, perhaps, with a negative word count. This isn't the time to give up hope—it's the time to slow down, to pay more attention, to spend more time. To sit with your work in stillness, putting aside your impatience and frustration, because the work can smell it, just as it can smell your fear and rage. If you were a small, shy creature, you wouldn't want to come out and play with a big person full of spiky negative emotions, either.

If you can do this, if you can attend to your beast with patience and faith, you will encounter the beautiful truth, which is that the mere fact of showing up will one day be enough. Your gentleness will coax that brilliant piece out. Perhaps it won't come out on your preferred timeline, but it will definitely come out on its own. Because every work of art has its own life span, its own needs, its own heartbeat; only if you take patient care of it over time will the work reveal these intimate things to you.

THE BEST PART IS THE DAYDREAMING

The daydreaming part of writing is so hard to define or explain, but it's as important as anything else we do. And it's also one of the most pleasurable parts.

I acknowledge that I'm talking about the importance of letting your mind wander from the position of a person who has the benefit of space. I live alone, which allows me to call on solitude whenever I please.

But I think you can find ways to claim your daydream space no matter your living or working situation. What does it truly require but some quiet? What do we need but a door to close? Even if it's metaphorically so: just to be alone with yourself, not to be required to speak to anyone else. It can be in public, on a park bench, or a chair on a street corner outside a café, looking at nothing in particular. In the midst of noise, too, it can happen. All the daydreams I had on a subway ride through Brooklyn in my life, on the way to work in the morning.

And I will say this till death, but: no computer, no phone, no distractions. Technology is not your brain, not this kind of brain. This is you summoning your truest, most creative part of yourself. It cannot be captured by anyone else, so you must capture it yourself.

And what can grasping at this daydream time get you? The humming of your brain. The operation of a pristine engine. That's what it feels like to me when I sit, dazed, nearly trancelike, and ponder whatever I'm working on. My brain feels warm, my chest feels warm. Things are in motion. If I'm writing fiction, sometimes to get things started, I close my eyes and try to picture myself in the same room as my characters. When I'm writing nonfiction, I visualize someone else listening to the story I'm trying to tell them. But usually I'm thinking about nothing at all, and then suddenly find myself arriving at a point.

And again, there is that feeling of moving words and sentences and paragraphs and ideas around in my head. It's soothing, to think about my work in this manner. All the possibilities, all the surprises, that can surface when you just let your mind wander.

If you can do it today, or tomorrow, or soon, walk away from the noise and the obligation, even if only for a little bit. Let your brain sing. No pen or paper necessary. Just the warm and tender feeling of letting your mind wander to wherever it needs to go.

ANDREW SEAN GREER

Imitation is part of creativity. A famous composer, a protégé of Leonard Bernstein, played his latest piece for an elderly Bernstein who, after listening, said, "It's Chopin. You don't need me anymore. You've learned how to steal." Or here's T. S. Eliot: "Immature poets imitate; mature poets steal; bad poets deface what they take, and good poets make it into something better, or at least something different."

So what does this mean? It means take your favorite scene from a novel and put it in yours, if only to learn how it functions. Is it still wonderful out of context? If it still works in yours, then there is something technical about the scene that works apart from the characters and setting—and that technical lesson is one you are free to steal. Told backward, or from a distance, or from the dog's point of view. Don't steal the content; steal the technique. Made wholly yours, it isn't theft—it's learning to read like a writer.

CAMILLE DUNGY

It feels odd to be tasked with writing words to help motivate folx to sit in the chair and write. I'm in a fallow phase right now. I don't feel inspired. It's cold outside. The plants are dormant. I have roughly 7,896 letters of recommendation to write plus some papers to grade. I think my muse has flown off to the Bahamas or someplace on an extended vacation. Whoever tells you that writing is fun must have a very different kind of life than the one I am living right now.

But I'm a Capricorn who feels compelled to meet deadlines and complete assignments, so here I am trying to honor this commitment. It's 12:20 in the afternoon, and I'm still in my insanely comfortable gray fleece onesie, having avoided my own writing project very effectively since I woke up six hours ago. There were so many things to do this morning, you see. This weekend I moved some furniture around in my study, and now I have a pile of books scattered over the floor. They need alphabetizing, but when I tried to shelve them, I realized there were some books on the shelf whose continued status in my most-favored-book shelf required re-evaluation. What makes a book a most-favored book, I asked myself, pausing my frantic motion to consider the question.

The candle my sister sent for my birthday three years ago filled my study with a smell similar to a balmy ocean breeze, if the smell of an ocean breeze could be contained in creamy white 100 percent organic wax.

I think my sister sent me that candle as an apology for not being in more regular touch. All those years we spent as girls together, living near the ocean neither of us live close to anymore. The candle has tiny seashells and smooth gray and speckled beach pebbles embedded in the wax. There's a bright silver plate affixed to the jar: "Thinking of you," it reads. I haven't put a flame anywhere near that candle's wick. Doubt I ever will. I don't want to burn up its beauty.

Sometimes it's okay to let beautiful things go unburned. Sometimes it's okay to let thoughts sit on the shelf of the mind for some length of time before we put them to "use" in our writing. Sometimes what seems like not using a thing or a thought is actually a matter of figuring out a better use for that thing or that thought than I might have originally imagined.

I lifted another book from the stack at my feet but put it back down just as quickly. I was very tired. I thought about how much I love the sheets I bought in the first months of the pandemic shutdowns, when I realized I'd be spending more time in bed. I'd never owned sheets so nice before. Like butter, people say about smooth things. I'd never understood that phrase so keenly until I spent a night with my skin pressed against the slick cool softness of those light blue sheets.

Maybe by now you can see what I'm doing. Maybe you understand that, though I didn't want to write today, I have managed to write. I am nearly five hundred words into something whose entirety hasn't revealed itself yet. I can say

I set a timer and typed, without stopping. I let my mind lead my fingers over the keyboard. I kept going. That's the main thing. As I wrote, I asked myself to stay in touch with my body, my mind. I engaged with my senses. Smell and touch in this case. And I moved into memory, too. Not particularly deeply. But I touched my toes in the water and left room to wade further in. I touched on some triggers for worry, for sadness, for nostalgia, for connection, for joy. I started to describe at least two different settings. You, reader, even know what the speaker is wearing in this scene and what time of day it is in her world.

There was a moment when I asked myself to smile. I stayed in touch with my body and told myself to smile and, as I smiled, my fingers typed a happy thought (that candle). And though the happy thought complicated itself almost instantly, there it is on the page, a moment of peace inside my murky morning. Now I have a life raft to return to in a future draft.

MEGAN GIDDINGS

So, I am not much of a quotes person. I am firmly against epigrams in a very superstitious way. I'm not willing yet to give someone more famous and smarter than me the first chance to speak in my novels! But I've been thinking a lot about a quote that I've seen attributed to many different people, most recently Viola Davis: "How you love defines your life." I know it might sound a little T.J. Maxx wall art to some of you, my more cynical friends in literature, but stay with me.

When I teach characterization, I tend to go back to Alice LaPlante's methods for building characters, for knowing if they're working on their page: speak, feel, act, react, think. I spend most of my time on *react* because it's the one easiest to forget, especially when we're writing and being solitary and the only part of us moving while writing tends to be our hands. Your characters' bodies, their processing, the things they suddenly do because their world has changed keep the story (the essay, the poem, the script) moving. To me, reactions tend to be when I know my characters. It's when the work comes to life.

But maybe today is the day we bring in a new element to our work. Today, especially if you're stuck in your writing,

I want you to ask yourself, "How does this character love?" How do they let themselves understand and receive other people's love? In many ways these past years, some of the predominant emotional stress to me has been these negotiations between how I give love and how people would prefer to receive it. And if love is too woo for you, go to one of the hardest elements of love, of being alive: What is your character's relationship to vulnerability? How do they express it? How do they react to it? How has it changed them? How has it changed you?

HOW TO FILL THAT WELL

I don't want to say I wake up automatically inspired every day, because there are some mornings when my brain only wants to think about going back to bed or eating or taking a walk or looking online to see if those shoes that I want have gone on sale yet.

But most days I awaken feeling at least a little inspired, letting ideas simmer and stew in the delicious broth of my morning brain. I'm usually ready to sit down and engage with my notebook in some manner, even if it's just a casual check-in with my mind, how I'm feeling as the sun rises, how the day looks to me through the window.

But what of the days I don't? What about when I feel like I have nothing to say, and yet, because this is what I do for a living, I must be inspired at least a little bit no matter what? I'm not saying the well is dry entirely or that I'm afraid I'll never fill it again, but I am keenly aware that *the well needs to be filled*.

So what do we do when we feel like we don't have anything to say? What do we do when the well is dry? How do we refill it?

I like to go to see art in a museum. On Wednesdays, the New Orleans Museum of Art is free to Louisiana residents. Sometimes I take a walk in a new part of town I've never been before, or I take a reverse walk from my usual path, so I can see everything from the other direction. I download an album from the year I was born, or the year I lost my virginity, or the year I sold my first book. I go to the garden shop and buy one small plant for my backyard, and then I dig a hole for it, and then I look at it from my desk window, and it reminds me that everything is alive in one way or another. I go to the café, and I eavesdrop on conversations and sometimes I write down what I hear just to remember what it feels like to do that if it's been a while. I flip to the beginning of my project and read through the first few pages and try to channel the moment I began writing it. How did

I feel the day I started it? What inspired me in the first place? What was so important to me then? Is it still now?

It usually is.

My friend Kristen Arnett likes to revisit well-worn favorite television shows and books she's seen or read a million times. Just to let herself enjoy them and remember why art makes her happy.

Sometimes I choose to visit different destinations that are within driving distance. A cool cemetery I've never visited before an hour away. A park in a different part of the city. And there are small trips we can take every day. A different route to the grocery store. A new block to explore. Or even a place to visit in your mind.

I remember taking a ride on the new ferry in New Orleans, from the edge of the French Quarter, across the Mississippi, to the West Bank. I took it with Anne Gisleson: we rode our bikes downtown in the summer heat, hopped on the ferry, then biked to her sister's house to say hello and take a dip in her pool. It was nice to see the city coming and going from the deck of the boat. The river is so wild and dangerous and has so much power, but we were riding safely atop it. A simple enough ritual, but it was meaningful to me, and repositioned my perspective a bit.

Not one action you can take will fill the well entirely. Often we need small spoonfuls to replenish it. But we must make the attempt. Drip by drop. We must try.

ISAAC FITZGERALD

"Can I move? I'm better when I move."

That line is spoken by Robert Redford playing the Sundance Kid in the Academy Award–winning 1969 film *Butch Cassidy and the Sundance Kid*.

I recommend watching the whole movie—it's one of my favorites—but it's not necessary to follow what I'm about to lay out.

What I'm trying to say is, I, too, am better when I move. Writing for me comes easier when I'm not sitting still. When I'm not in one place. When I'm moving through the world, instead of trying to force the world to come to me.

Now, I am of course familiar with that old saying, "Get your ass in the chair and write." I don't know who said it first, and it's not bad advice. The catch is, for me, if my ass has already been sitting in a chair—or on the couch, or in bed, or on a barstool—*not* writing, well . . . not much is going to come from my ass being in the chair when it *is* time to write.

But if I've been walking, if I've taken some time to move my body—which more importantly is about opening my mind up to the outside world—then when it comes time to write I find that the words come more easily.

So try this on for size: before you write your 1000 words today, maybe take 1000 steps. Or do that yoga video you've been putting off. Or even simply meditate—which is to say allow your mind to move if you ain't so interested in movement of the body.

Or maybe it's less "you ain't so interested" and more "due to health reasons you can't."

Writer and walker extraordinaire Garnette Cadogan once said to me, "I think of walking as much more than 'one step in front of the other.' I think of people moving in wheelchairs as walkers. What I fundamentally mean when I say 'walking' is 'moving at human pace.' Moving through the world and absorbing the world in its rich detail. At human pace. At human scale."

We're all better when we move, whatever "move" means to you. We're all better when we absorb the world at a "human pace."

So if you have the time, get out into the world a bit today. Or simply break up your routine. Try not writing at your desk. Or write at a different time of day than you usually do. My way of doing this is to go for a walk, during which I always have a notebook stuck in my back pocket. That way, I can sit on a park bench and write. Or in a bar. Or a restaurant. Or on the beach. Or in a field. Anywhere, really. A new place to sit and scribble always helps me put words down on the page.

Which reminds me, while I have you, another bit of advice—at least something that works for me—is writing longhand. When I'm staring at a blank computer screen, the enormity of filling that screen with perfectly placed words can be overwhelming. I stop at every single mistake (there are so many) and try to correct it immediately. I can't move on from the sentence I just wrote without doing my damnedest to make it impeccable, which really just means I don't get much writing done at all. But when I start scratching a pen on a piece of paper, my spelling mistakes don't matter, my switch of tenses can be fixed later, my grammar remains horrendous, but that's okay. There's a forward movement, one word after the other. Then, when I transcribe my chicken scratch from the written page to my computer, that's when I can get some editing done. When I can start fixing my mistakes. But the words are there, thank goodness. The words are already there.

No matter what you decide to do, no matter how you write your words, mix it up a little bit today, that's all I ask. Move. Move through the world—or your apartment or simply your mind—as Garnette put it, "at a human pace." Then put your ass in the chair, wherever that chair may be, and write.

Happy hunting. Maybe I'll see you out there.

READING YOUR WORK OUT LOUD

There was a spring I gave a reading from a new book I was writing and it felt great to do it. It energized me. I woke up the next morning and thought, *I need to work on this book.* I want to have more of that feeling. Of putting my fiction out into the world. Of being heard in that way.

It was rejuvenating. The public uttering of my words made me want to dig in and get my hands dirty again.

It wasn't just the reading it out loud part. It was the imagining of an audience, the preparation for it, the practicing, the intense edits I gave my work up until the last second. (Picture me scribbling frantically on my printout right before I was called on stage.) But then, yes, to hear my words out loud, too, as if they were somehow alive and not just in my head, or in my notebook, or on this cursed screen.

Do you ever read your work out loud to anyone? Could you read it to a friend on the phone or over Zoom? Are there open mic nights available in your city? Could you even set up a reading in your living room or in a park?

For years now I have hosted readings in my home. First in my apartment in Brooklyn, where we would all wander up to the roof afterward to watch the sunset across the river over Manhattan, and now in my backyard, in New Orleans, where the readings have to be finished before it gets dark and the bugs come out. Afterward the author stands in my garden and signs books and talks to each and every person. I love bringing people together, creating a space for them to connect in real life and hear the written word out loud. Boy, does it keep me alive. I view it all as an incredible artistic exchange.

But we are all working with our limitations, I know. And often rules we didn't create, and that are ever-changing. So if your answer to all of this is, "No, I cannot"—I understand. Not everyone wants to get up in front of someone else and read, not everyone wants to meet in real life. That idea can be intimidating, and I totally get it.

It used to terrify me, reading in public. I made it a New Year's resolution many years ago to get over my fears, and I forced myself to do open mic nights in small bars on the Lower East Side until I could finally feel comfortable. My whole body used to shake: legs, backside, hands. I'm sure I looked a little ridiculous. I raced through my reading till the end. But each time it got a little better. Each time I shook a little less.

Even if public presentations aren't possible for you to access, maybe it's just about showing someone—anyone, truly—your work if you've been afraid to in the past. Maybe it's about constructing that audience for yourself in your head and imagining what it would feel like to have them hear your words.

When does the liftoff come where the words are not just for you but for someone else, too? And how can that line of thinking transform your work? You can write for yourself forever, and that's fine, they're your words! But what does contemplating an audience for a moment do to them? What happens when the work evolves to a place where it's suddenly for everyone?

HANNAH TINTI

When I was younger, I did pottery. Before I learned how to throw on the wheel, or fire a kiln, or even how to press a pinch pot, my teacher showed us how to make clay. There was a huge barrel of slip in the studio, a trash can filled with water, where everyone would throw their mistakes. Any failed creation (that hadn't been baked yet) would be recycled back into mud, and the first step to making new clay was to grab a heavy shovel and start tossing these old mistakes into the giant mixer. Every once in a while, we'd open the lid and check the consistency. If the clay was too dry, we'd throw in another shovel of failure.

This is how I've come to think of first drafts. Before you can make a priceless vase or a heartfelt novel, you've got to make the clay. And you better put on some overalls, because you're going to get covered with muck. The good news is, you can recycle some of your old ideas. In fact, using the slurry of previous work ages your clay (like fine wine in an oak barrel), making it stronger and more flexible, which greatly increases the chances that your next creation won't end up in the slip bucket. So think of your 1000 words today as raw material. It doesn't have to look like anything yet. But one day you'll come back to it and spin it into something beautiful.

ONCE I WHISPERED TO MYSELF

―

Write without fear. Perhaps you know this too, but I shall say it one more time. Whisper it to yourself whenever you waver from your intention. Write without fear.

HOW TO FIND THE TIME

I get up early every day, around six, sometimes earlier, because this is the time that works best for my brain. I make a cup of coffee, I feed the dog and let him out back. Then I sit in my big blue chair in the back office with a notebook and begin to write. I do this because good ideas pop up when you least expect it. We cannot begin without the ideas. Sometimes an idea shows up that has nothing to do with what I'm working on, and I write it down on a scrap of paper, and then a few months later or even a year later I see it again, but really I'm seeing it for the first time, in a way that seems recognizable and informative and rife with possibility.

Even if I'm not even working on a particular project I sit down and make the time. I find it very freeing; I tend to be more experimental when I write by hand. Sometimes I'm not even aware I've begun a book because I'm always in a state of writing, and I wonder if what I'm working on my entire life is, in a way, one long book, everything is just another chapter—but that's for another discussion.

The point is, I get it together early in the morning in preparation for not just now but the future, too. It's worth it to try to find the time.

The most successful time of day for me to write is in the morning, not only because my brain works best then but because it's my best shot at being free of distractions. But this might not be the case for you. We all have different patterns, different circadian rhythms. For some people their creative selves don't even come out until it's well past midnight.

And we have all kinds of claims on our time in life. Some of us have families, or demanding jobs, or jobs with unpredictable schedules, or we're caregivers to loved ones in addition to our jobs, or we have health issues. All of this can add up to not enough time for yourself, let alone for your work. One thousand words a day may not be possible. It's just a number. But I bet two hundred words might be possible for you. Or five hundred.

Write what you can, when you can.

Write when the urge strikes you, but also, be disciplined. Carve out time in your day to write. Fight for that time for yourself. You can find holes in your schedule. They exist. And soon enough you will fill them with words.

MICHAEL WEBER

Here's something you probably already know: it's too easy to avoid writing.

So my advice is to be hard on yourself about finding the time to write—extremely hard—but then be kind to yourself after that. Don't worry about quality. Just put the time in, day after day. Make writing more important than other things in your life. Because anyone can write when they feel like it, when they have a good idea, when they're not sick or hungover or tired. I recommend writing when you don't feel like it, when you have no good ideas, when you couldn't be more busy and have a hundred reasons not to write. Turn writing into something you have to do.

My self-esteem is tied to my productivity. If I don't write, I don't feel good about myself. I'm no longer scared to write poorly because the worst feeling is not writing at all.

CELESTE NG

I am a perfectionist by nature so the drafting stage is hard for me. It is really hard to just move forward and put something down on paper because part of my brain is always screaming, "But it's not quite right! Erase it! Erase it NOW!"

But I've also learned that it is very rare to get something completely right on the first try—and that it's approximately nine million times easier to revise something from "not great" into "actually kind of decent." So for me, the key is getting something down, and even when it's imperfect—which is always—it usually points me in the direction I need to dig in.

Over the years, I've collected a bunch of analogies for the writing process that help me override that type-A instinct in my brain, at least temporarily. In *Bird by Bird*, Anne Lamott talks about the first draft being the "down draft" (just get it down), and the second draft being the "up draft" (when you fix it up).

And then there's a sign I have over my writing desk, which I glance up at as needed. It just says "WORRY ABOUT THAT LATER."

THE THING YOU LOVE TO DO

You can do it today, and tomorrow, and the next day too, and every day for the rest of your life. Get up a little early every morning, pull out the notebook, and scratch on it until you're done. Or stay up late, when the house is real quiet, and then write till your fingers bleed. No one will ever stop you from doing any of this. No one else can get in your way but you. Push all the voices in your head aside. For this is the thing you love and need to do.

ELIZABETH McCRACKEN

The older I get the less I know—which is common enough, but also the less I know about myself as a writer. I used to believe I had to be tricked into being productive, because naturally I'm a lazy person. Probably that's still true and I'm now easier to trick and also increasingly naïve about my own naïveté. One foolproof rule is to hitch your wagon to the hardest-working writers you know, people you love who are highly productive. I've always worked harder so as not to resent my beloved workhorses.

Writers love to give advice about writing because they enjoy talking to themselves; all writerly advice is just that, advice to self, appeals for validation, self-mythologizing, self-soothing, all of it necessary if you want to get any work done. As for me, I cannot plan things out before I write. The bigger the project is, the less I plan. If I had to know everything before I started, I would never start, because I really only think in language. I can only make decisions while actually writing. It's the work itself that's the lantern I swing to see ahead in the darkness, the words and sentences and paragraphs I get down that let me see where I'm going. I remind myself that no first draft can be perfect, but also that

I'm allowed to show off, to take pleasure in turns of phrase and private jokes, to digress. Novel writing for me requires a lot of privacy, partly because I'm so insufferable in early drafts, so full of swagger and ambition and burlesque. I give myself permission for everything. I give you who are reading this permission, too.

(I am talking to myself.)

WILL LEITCH

Every writer has their favorite quote about writing, and, fittingly, my favorite one is more about the process of writing rather than any sort of deep artistic fulfillment. The quote comes from Roger Ebert: "The muse visits during the act of creation, not before."

As usual, this is Ebert—a blue-collar newspaper guy at his core—saying something practical and vital in a lovelier way than most of us would say it: He's saying shut up and work. One of the most difficult things about writing is overcoming all the excuses we give ourselves *not* to write: we're not feeling inspired, we haven't figured out what we want to say, we're pretty sure the computer is blinking meanly at us over there. What Ebert is saying is that writing, the physical act of hitting letter keys with your fingers, is the vessel for inspiration: You don't know what you have to say until you say it.

I grew up as a writer in the online world where your job, a job not all that different from Ebert's newspaper work, is to fill a box, hit save, and then go fill another one. To many, this has made words feel more disposable, but I found it freeing: I couldn't swim around in my own head because there was no time. The box had to be filled. Now that my writing is less deadline driven, I try to keep the same approach: *Just make shit*. I have all the time in the world to go fix it later: The hardest part is getting it down the first time. I'm able to be productive because I don't think of writing as something that happens in my head. It's a physical act. It's building a shelf. It's work. It's making something that didn't exist before. Get out of your head. Fill the box. Go make shit.

DEEP LISTENING

Living through a natural disaster has nothing to do with writing. I'm pretty good at always thinking about writing, but I didn't consider it much during Hurricane Ida in New Orleans. Instead, I thought about my friends and my community and my dog and finding a way to get in touch with people because my wireless service no longer worked. I thought about how long I should stay in my house, how bad things might get, and where I could go when I left. Though my house protected me from the storm, it could not protect me from what came after. Though I loved this city more than any other, I didn't feel safe there. I felt like I would be someone who would end up needing help rather than being able to provide it.

The morning after the storm I woke up energized by adrenaline. I got on my bike and rode all over the place and saw all the destruction, and I ran into a neighbor and then another, and we all assessed our personal damage with each other. It was hot and the sun was strong, and we had no power. People were kind to each other, offered food and water, but it was hard not to be riled up. I kept saying, "I'm rattled." Finally, I ran into another neighbor who had internet service and through him I was able to ask for help from generous friends outside of the state who secured me housing. I was lucky and privileged to have had a car with a full tank of gas and the freedom to go. Many others were not.

I left early in the morning after a sleepless night, in the darkness, in the heat; I packed up my car and drove through a city in blackout, no streetlights, no traffic lights, no nothing, except for my car, and I can't even describe to you what it looked like because it was just dark and darker, and I held my breath until I hit the highway and it was still dark for a good long while after that, in the sky and in the sprawling city and beyond. I didn't think, *How will I write about this in the future?* I didn't think, *How will I structure this into three acts?* I didn't think, *What lessons can be taken from this moment?* I only thought, *How do I get out of town and to the next place safely?*

I didn't think: Pay attention, because this will be important someday . . . which I sometimes say to myself when something new or big or weird or dramatic or scary or sad is happening. I didn't have to say any of that to myself because I already knew I wouldn't forget. I'm so good at making everything about writing, but this only had to do with living.

But there was this one thing I can share with you.

Lately I have become fascinated with deep listening. I have a character I've been developing who works with music and sounds, and so sometimes I try to think like her, and I sit somewhere and take note of all the different noises around me, and try to imagine what it would be like to hear things distinctly like that all the time, to not have to pay attention to it so specifically like I do; to have it come naturally. It's a good and interesting exercise.

I found once the power went out during the hurricane and as I sat in the darkness, all I could think about were the sounds. That was what was left for me. I sat in my living room with one candle flickering and I just listened. The wind was ceaseless for hours, whining and aggressive, and there was rain, too, no thundering, just pounding rain against the doors and walls and windows. And I could hear glass breaking in surrounding houses, shatters here and there, and also siding and roof tiles blowing off and occasionally banging against my house. Also there was this popping noise—I had thought at first it was a transformer blowing, it was that kind of sound, like a sudden explosion of electricity—but it happened over and over again all night long, and I thought, *Maybe when I go out in the morning it will still be happening so I will know what it was.* But I never found out.

Then the security alarm went off at the house next door and stayed on through the night, and I slept with a pillow over my head, and it nearly drowned out the sound but not quite. And there was more rain, too, that stayed after the wind left, just violent and ceaseless. For a while it felt like it would rain forever, that all I would ever know again was the sound of that rain.

All the sounds were separate for me, but of course they were all together, too, part of a grand composition. A hurricane symphony.

We must live in the moment when we need to be present for ourselves, our neighbors, the world around us. Seek safety, take care. But right now, I ask you to consider all the sounds around you, to sit quietly and engage in some deep listening. Or think about some unforgettable noises you've heard in the past. To see what—if any— impact it can have on your work. I offer you my experience to help you consider the sounds around you. All the symphonies we hear in our lives.

THE BOOKS WE GATHER FOR SAFETY

There are times when the pages can feel foreign to you, too far away from your present tense. It's important to realize when you're not being honest on the page. You're not lying, but you're not telling the truth either—but why? For me, it's because I feel unsafe or insecure. And I need a sense of those two things to put myself in the place where I can be vulnerable.

When this happens, sometimes I gather up a stack of books that I return to all the time. Some of these books have directly influenced my writing, and others have just provided me with comfort or entertainment. I return to them for strength and inspiration. The authors had lived deeply in these pages so that they could write them. Even if there were uncomfortable moments contained within the books, these stories were told so beautifully and openly that I took comfort in them. I felt as if I had gathered a group of old friends around me. I found the safety. But also, I found a challenge: I couldn't lie to them, put anything past them. If they were honest in their words, I had to be honest in mine.

What are the books that make you feel safe? Can you gather them around you today?

MY MANTRA

My mantra for a few years now has been this: Stay in it.

When you are at your desk or kitchen table or couch or back porch or bed, or wherever it is you are writing these days, think to yourself: Stay in it. Stay on the page. Stay in the room, stay in the scene, stay in the moment, stay in the idea. Stay in the sentence. Stay in your words. Stay in it.

Close your browser window, open whatever medium you write in/on, and get to work. Do not blink, do not think twice, do not scroll in the other open windows one last time, because whatever you think you will find there, it will still be waiting when you are done. Do nothing else but write. Let it pour out of you. If it feels urgent, use it. Be there on the page. Now.

Stay in the work, until it's done.

MAURICE RUFFIN

For me, getting the writing done comes down to the two Fs: fun and flexibility. The other day I was talking to a class of sixth-grade writers. One of the students asked me, "Do you ever throw away any writing?" I told her of course I do because that's a sign that I'm doing something right. Every time I write something lengthy, say, over twenty-five pages, I get lost like I'm in a maze. I wander around typing random words. I have that where-did-I-put-my-keys feeling. But I've figured out that I only get lost when I'm not enjoying what I'm writing. Eventually, I ask myself, "What would I rather be writing if I wasn't afraid to switch over to a new idea or approach?" That's when I switch over.

It's a heart-wrenching moment to put down something I was invested in for something I haven't even started. Like swinging from a trapeze and hoping your partner catches you. Yet, they usually catch me. It often turns out that the initial project was just throat clearing. The writing gods were scoping me out to see if I was serious about wanting to write something special. The new thing always feels like a jailbreak. I'm free free free to drop my tools and run for freedom. I have all new characters, new settings, new ideas, and in this phase I tend to write two or three times faster than before. The getaway car is driving itself and I just try to hang on. It's so dangerous and so crazy, but it's so fun, which is the main reason I write anyway.

WRITING THE WRONG WAY
TO GET TO THE RIGHT WAY

My friend Zach Lazar, author of eight novels and professor at Tulane University, never throws anything away. He writes as sloppy and fast as he can, then he circles the good stuff and cuts the rest. He always thinks about being less linear. "You think the sentences should go in a certain order, but they don't necessarily need to. I move them around into a different order, and then get rid of what doesn't work," he says.

Helpful, I thought, when he told me that. Extremely helpful. He said it casually, because he'd been doing it forever. That out-of-order trick. Couldn't hurt. They're just sentences, after all. Throwing away something that "works" and seeing what's left behind. Or maybe put a few sentences in a new, weird pile, or write against the assignment or what's expected of you? Move the end to the beginning or vice versa? What a relief it is to mess things up. Forget your glasses, answer the wrong question. What a relief it might be to do it wrong.

COCKTAIL PARTY

—

One of my favorite writing tricks is to pretend
I'm gossiping about the people I'm writing about.
I imagine I'm standing in the center of a group
of people at a party whom I'm trying to impress
with my storytelling and wit. So I better be interesting as hell.

RACHEL SYME

I have a photograph that I keep over my desk of the late
writer Jacqueline Susann gabbing on a white rotary telephone. In the picture, Susann is wearing a short, gauzy
peignoir nightgown, glitter-dusted house slippers and, im-
pressively, a full set of lashes despite being otherwise dressed
for a night in. She is leaning back in a desk chair with her
feet flung up onto a bookshelf, and she is beaming. I do not
know exactly when the photograph was taken, but it must
be from sometime in the 1960s, the decade when Susann
transformed herself from a failed actress into the kind of
splashy literary celebrity who sits for author portraits in her
pajamas. Susann's first bestseller was a 1963 book called
Every Night, Josephine! about her rambunctious standard
poodle (the *Marley and Me* of the *Mad Men* set), but it was
Valley of the Dolls, her 1966 potboiler about three striving
New York gals and the pills they pop, that made her a house-
hold name and moved millions of copies. She wrote the
book quickly and sloppily; according to her editor, she typed
her drafts on pale pink paper in all capital letters with ec-
centric punctuation, and "added revisions in a large, forceful
circular hand, with what looked like a blunt eyebrow pencil."

She didn't really think too much about structure or narrative consistency—those were pesky problems to solve later—and instead she pecked out frothy, zingy passages about sex and showbiz, catfights and callous men, barbiturates and barbed bitchy asides. Is the book . . . good? Is it . . . camp? I don't know that Susann gave either question much thought. She did not have the time. In 1962, Susann learned that she had late-stage, terminal breast cancer and that she had perhaps a decade to live (she made it twelve more years). She wrote all her bestsellers under the heel of this knowledge. Right before her mastectomy surgery, which she had before she wrote any books at all, she wrote in her diary, "I can't die without leaving something—something big."

I keep this photograph above my desk for a few reasons: To remind myself we are all writing against the clock, whether or not we know how long we have. To remind myself that a person who wrote "I *think* I can write" in fact went on to write one of the top-selling books of the entire twentieth century (and at lightning speed—she churned out words at about the pace you are doing so now). But it also reminds me not to take writing so *seriously*. I don't know if you've read *Valley* recently but . . . the book is a total blast. It contains phrases like "New York was steaming—an angry concrete animal" and "Broadway doesn't go for booze and dope! Now get out of my way, I've got a man waiting for me." It is, in every way, a book that feels like a hot bubble bath in the summer: indulgent, irrational, a little nauseating. But it struck a chord because it was *fun*, and because Susann clearly had fun writing it. She lived in a glamorous hotel on Central Park West (ah, the days when people lived in hotels! She had a tuna fish sandwich brought up by room service every day so she could write through lunch!) and she wore Pucci everywhere and her husband was her publicist and together they had an extremely good time making her famous. Susann never talked about writing as a struggle; she clearly had bigger, more existential fish to fry. If anything, she infuriated everyone else who chiseled out sculptural sentences and felt deeply invested in literary quality (Truman Capote, for instance, shit-talked her on every late-night program he could book). She was everything that was wrong with books! She wore marabou and wiglets! But she enjoyed what she made, and, more importantly, she made something that people truly enjoyed.

I think that we all want to write something *great*. That's why we sit down at the desk, isn't it? Be honest. You want to be Herman Melville or Truman Capote, not Jacqueline Susann (or at least you want to be the Capote who wrote *In Cold Blood* and not the one who ultimately alienated all his socialite friends by writing a *very Valley*-esque novel). But what if you threw that idea out the window, just for today? What if, instead, you tried to have a good time? I know, writing is torturous. It often feels bad and useless. To quote Nora Ephron, "The hardest thing about writing is writing." But the real drug that keeps me coming back, I've found, is not the moments when I know I'm writing well. It's that 1 percent of the time when I'm having so much delirious fun that it feels indecent; when I feel like a kid again because I am click-clacking out words to please myself and not thinking at all about the outcome. I'll chase that 1 percent forever, even if it comes around once a year, or even once every few years. My favorite writing I've ever done is about the silliest topics—perfume, kitchen gadgets, caftans, high-waisted jeans, trashy Hollywood tell-alls—mostly because the more low-stakes I think something is when I approach it, the more I can just get out of my own way and start riffing. And maybe within the riffing, there are two or three sentences that sing, and maybe one of them is a keeper.

So I suppose my advice to you—and like most writing advice, you can take it or leave it—is to try to have a bit more silly, frothy, heady joy today when you sit down to write. What would you really *like* to write about? Pick anything! Anything at all!! It doesn't have to be something that connects to the current project. It's better if it doesn't! If it is great, you'll find a way to use it later, I promise. The goal is to produce a pleasurable little scrap of writing, a few buttery, flaky paragraphs that are just for you. Maybe it's a meditation on an old leather jacket. Maybe it's a menu of new cocktails you invent on the spot. Maybe it's a gossipy email to an old friend. Maybe it's a list of things you have languishing in various online shopping carts. Maybe it's a description of a truly disgusting smell. Maybe it's a few paragraphs about how summer feels in your hometown. Maybe it's a collection of random facts about dead famous people that you like to break out at parties. Maybe it's an argument in favor of a particular brand of seltzer. Maybe it's a short story you invent about whoever you can see outside your window right now. Maybe it's a fake DM conversation between clandestine lovers. Maybe it's a rant about a disappointing hamburger. Maybe it's a celebration of your grandmother's excessive teaspoon collection. Maybe it's a scene about a nightclub performer who has a full nervous breakdown in the street (wait, Jacqueline Susann already did that).

It can be silly! It *should* be silly! I am not telling you not to believe in your work, or not to believe that your work can be powerful, meaningful, and can change hearts and minds. But I am telling you that sometimes, to get to the gooey center, you need to spend a day on the chocolate shell. You need to wear glittery flats and have long aimless conversations on the phone and write something frivolous while twirling a cord around your almandine nails. Trust that it will all add up to something. The goofy writing days can be just as fruitful as the hard ones, and sometimes you need the former to crack the latter. Believe it or not, if you can find joy in your own writing, readers will feel it. They can sense the exact sentences where you were having a good time. Be a little ridiculous today.

MORGAN PARKER

This will be my first 1000 words of summer and I am fucking terrified. I am going to fail. Whatever my goals are, I will not reach them. I will no t create award-winning literature . I will break many of my own intentions and lose at least two days bullying myself and at least one day coddling myself, and I definitely won't finish my book. Like, let's be real, Morgan. It's 2 weeks. So I'm going to forgive myself upfront for failing to meet my own absurd expectations, and congratulate m self ahead of time for returning, each day, to"the desk", willfully and intentionally, gratefully and purposefully, because that is how it happens. And something ~~will~~ will happen.

Before counting anything I would like to congratulate myself for all the days when 20 feels like Everest. When I hate 1,000 out of 1,000 of my words. I'm forgiving myself in advance for all the absolute crap I will write before getting my groove. For taking too many TV breaks. For not getting to The Desk before 5pm. I will get my head out of my ass and my mind out of my head, and eat meals and ~~██████~~ drink water. I will be too dedicated to doubt myself and too ~~████████~~ imaginative to judge myself. I will not delete sentences before finishing them. When the phone or the dog whines for my attention I will finish my thought first. If the computer woos me with its wiki research wormholes or sneers at me with its sassy cursor, I will switch to a notebook. If I find myself doodling, I'll move to a typewriter. I will show my tools some love (just ify my indulgences); be in love with the p hysical "stuff" of craft. Limited edition pencils, pocket fountain pens, German typewriters with fresh ribbons, gifted note-books, special pencil sharpener, red pens and green staples. I will de-intellectualize and re-sensualize my writing practice. Pay attention to how my body feels. The whisper of a scrawling hand sliding over paper. The bell at the end of the line. Turning a new page. I will turn a new page. When I find myself writing a grocery list I will make a snack. When my wrists hurt I'll take a walk. When Netflix asks i fI'm still watching, I will leave the house altogether.When I don't remember what I'm doing or why, I'll read June Jordan poems, Baldwin's Art of Fiction interview, and if necessary 8th grade journals or the high school essay that concludes "I will write." Back then I said it was the only thing I knew for certain. Today's a new moon, maybe that's why I'm writing intentions. I am trying to be an affirmation for myself. This morning I set an alarm for 4:30am ~~████~~ with the label "the moon is new". When it woke me I rose up in bed and wondered if I should go outside and look. ~~██████████████████~~

ON FAVORS

When I have asked these wonderful authors to write these letters for me over the last five years, I was asking for a favor. I was asking them to give me their time and words on behalf of other people. To be present and part of this community and dip into their wells of knowledge and their feelings about their work and the world around them. Sometimes these feelings are very clear and sometimes they are clouded or complicated. Sometimes these people are busy. Sometimes the last fucking thing they want to do is think or talk about their work. (And they can say no.) (And I won't take it personally.)

What I'm trying to get at is that it's an "ask," as they say, to invite someone to write one of these letters, and when they say yes, it's a gift, and I couldn't appreciate it more. I don't take it lightly when they say yes to me. It's deep and meaningful when they agree to loan me their words for this project. They are showing up for me as much as they are showing up for everyone who participates in this community. Because they understand what it's like to be part of something bigger than themselves.

What does it mean to ask someone for help or an act of service in this world of writing? In any kind of world? It's always important to consider what we're asking someone to do not just in the context of our life but in the context of their lives. What is their time and energy worth? What does it mean to show up for someone else on the page, or in person, creatively, professionally? When we exchange services with each other, we're cultivating community. And sometimes we must do it without expecting anything in return.

We are all just taking turns looking out for each other in this life. This much I know. These writers give me their words, I pass them on to you, maybe you share them with someone else. These favors both big and small that keep us all creatively alive.

KIESE LAYMON & JAMI ATTENBERG

Dear Jami,

I kept thinking of who I should write a real-fake-real letter to and I decided it should be to the person who asked me to write a letter in the first place. I'm on my way back to Houston. Whenever I think of Houston, I feel New Orleans. Whenever I feel New Orleans, I think of your work on and off the page to make this little space we get before we die bolder and much more tender.

Not sure if you remember inviting some of us to a reading at your home in New York years ago. It was packed. I kept wondering how it felt to sleep in a home filled with stories after we left. I was so scared but also so so thankful that a writer whose skills I feared and imitated wanted other writers in their house. That's the thing about your work; even this request was for writers to come over to play in a space you're caring for.

And while I'm thankful, I'm trying to understand what to do with this post-memoir and post-pandemic personal desire to never ever share a space like that with anyone, especially writers who I love, again.

I'm so scared of people, Jami. I'm so disappointed in us. And I'm asking you if you feel this feeling much. I avoid people now at all costs. I'm just terrified of who we are, who I am, and I wonder how to do the work we have chosen while being terrified of people and petrified of their touch. This letter has far more to do with money and intimacy and feeling good than I'm comfortable writing, but if you want to write back, can you tell me if you still love people?

Do you have to love people to have them over to read? I feel like you have to love people to request a letter. Maybe you have to love people to respond to that request with a misanthropic confession. I'm scared of writing well about who we have become because I don't want to discover that this is who we have always been.

This is who we have always been.

Jami, do you have to love people to have them over to read?

Kiese

My friend Kiese,

Had to lean over at the table I was sitting at when I got this email because I felt this in my gut. It is hard to be out in the world, has been, will be, forever.

I will start off by saying: You're so full of love every day in my eyes. I think of you, and I think love. So I love people, and I love you, and I believe (know) that you love, too.

I think about that reading you gave at my loft in Brooklyn all the time because I've rarely seen a room light up with so much excitement, especially for a person they were meeting and hearing for the first time. It was everything I hoped for. You sold out of all your books that day, and you snuck out early. You have been sneaking out early forever.

I think anyone can sleep in a house full of stories just by surrounding themselves with books. But I have always been charged and changed—for better and for worse—by the energy of people. I only invite people to read if I love them, love their work, yes. But also I have to think their work feels necessary to the kind of audience that would come to my home or anywhere I might set up a reading. The kind of writers who are directly in conversation with their audience. Which I think you are.

The hard part of having that conversation, though, is sometimes it lifts us up and sometimes it takes something out of us. Beyond the thoughts of sharing air and space with people in this post-pandemic world: It is hard to receive attention, to stand in front of a room full of people. Last night I gave a reading of some of the letters from this project, this book, to a group of people, and I found myself saying, "This is corny." I felt drained as I read it. But afterward people said to me that people need inspiration, and that they wanted to go home and write. So if inspiration is corny, I'm in.

I have been disappointed by people my entire life, mostly by men. Still, people surprise me all the time. When I think about the work that I (we) do, the writing, the reaching out, the connecting, I think maybe it's for right now, and maybe it's for the people coming up behind us, too, and maybe even the people who were ahead of us, in a way. I'm just living every day on the page, and the page is eternal. This is who we've always been, you're right, it's bad, but also I know you know that there's good out there, too.

The question I have for you is this: Where and how can you find joy in your writing instead of being scared to write? Just for you, a gift for you. I wonder what you loved about it first, when you were young. You write for so many, but when do you get to write for you?

You don't have to touch anyone ever again but I will still ask you for a hug when I see you.

Jami

6
FALL

There are two questions I ask myself repeatedly about my writing until I'm so far along in a project I don't need to ask them anymore. They are:

1. Who are you writing this for?
2. What do you hope to accomplish with this work?

It's truly the best way to check in with yourself when you sit down to write. When the page feels at its blankest, you can immediately fill it by answering those questions.

Who is this for? What do I want it to do?

Sometimes the answers are:

1. Me.
2. So I cannot hate myself today.

And sometimes the answers are:

1. One specific person whom I'm writing at directly like a meteor headed toward Earth.
2. I want to do new things with perspective I've never done before because that sounds fun and interesting and is frankly kind of a turn-on.

And also:

1. My friends.
2. To impress the hell out of them, or at least make them laugh.

Or sometimes the answers are:

1. Everyone.
2. To make people feel less alone in the world.

I could keep going, because there's never a wrong answer, and they are all mostly true all the time. The thing I always return to after this brief and simple exercise is that making art of any kind is an act of optimism. To make art is to traffic in beliefs. The belief that you have something to say, that it's important to say it. And also the belief that someone specific might want to witness it in some way and gain something from it.

Every day I wake up and write my way into believing in myself and the world around me. I ask the questions, and the answers that I need are there. And with them, I can create at least a sliver of urgency.

This works even if I haven't done what I needed to yet. Even if my fears and patterns have gotten in the way of me getting work done. Or worse: if the world or my life has gotten in the way of it. I can always return to these questions. We will always have moments when we are more still or our days are less fruitful than we would like, especially in contrast to coming out of moments of extreme productivity.

But we can always return to the why, and forgive ourselves, and move on to the next. We have that power within us. For when we are ready.

WHEN THE CRISIS WINS

I can sit here and write about the pandemic and say it was an extraordinary historical moment where many of our lives shifted if not only in terms of physical or mental health or relationships but also in how and where we work. It happened on a grand scale. But there will always be one life event or another that can distract you. Be prepared for this. I don't live in fear of this but merely accept it as the truth. No one lives an entire life without a crisis at some point or another. And this may distract you from your daily practice.

After a family member was diagnosed with dementia, every time I visited them, I found it threw me off my work for a few days, if not longer. Eventually I began to find myself rushing to finish work before a family visit so I wouldn't fall behind afterward. Because I knew I would need time to decompress, and I would not be able to be my best creative self. I thought, *There is nothing I can do to change this moment of time in all our lives, and I need to be as present as possible.* Something had to give, and work was it. I didn't like how it affected me, but I had no choice. I, like you, am only human.

What I do not recommend is being angry with yourself for not getting your work done. None of us need to make ourselves feel bad twice. All we would be doing is building yet another hurdle for ourselves. Most of us need to feel comfortable, relaxed, and at ease in order to work, or at least able to trick our brains into feeling that way for a period of time. Being in a moment of crisis, and then being angry at yourself for being in that moment of crisis, will make it even harder to get work done. Everything takes time. And the work will be waiting for you when you are ready for it.

The crisis is temporary. Your work will be there for you forever.

MELISSA FEBOS

Today, I woke up at 5:50 a.m. to go for a long run and then to write. Let me be clear: I am not a morning person, have never been a morning person. I am a person who likes to putter and fuss and think and list and read deep into the night. However, since NYC has been sheltering in place and my partner and I have been stuck inside our two-bedroom apartment in Brooklyn, the early morning is the safest time to go for a long run outside—before there are people swarming the park and sidewalks in various degrees of maskedness or unmaskedness. So, I have forced myself to get up much earlier than my body prefers and to my surprise, I have fallen madly in love with the early morning. It is so *quiet*. It is the most still that I feel in a day. I have never seen the streets of my city as empty as they are these days at 6:00 a.m. Lately, they have been strewn with the hand-drawn signs of those who spent their evening demanding justice for Black lives.

For the first few weeks of homeboundedness, I was too overcome by despair and a sense of nihilism to write. Now, I have returned to the work, and it is waking something in me, as it has done so many times before. At this point in my life, I cannot separate my writing practice from my psychic survival. It is as necessary to me as any of the other things I do to avoid destroying myself or being consumed by the extreme fuckery of human life on this planet, among them therapy, running, twelve-step meetings, truly intimate connections with humans and other animals, and actions to manifest the world I want to live in. Writing ranks at the top of that list. It is simultaneously a place I go for respite and a place I go to find myself and what I think and feel about the world. So, I always find a way to come back to it.

When I was struggling to return to the page, I was dogged by the question *Who cares?* It is always a relevant question, but in this case, it was an expression of my own failure to imagine a near future where anyone gave a shit about any of the ideas that I'd had before things got to their present intensity. It was helpful for me to ask myself: What do *you* care about right now? Or, what are you curious about right now? Because under my feelings of anxiety, dread, anger, and helplessness, curiosity always remains—sometimes I just have to grope around a bit to find it. While I no longer felt curious about most of my own pre-pandemic ideas, there was one that still sparked my interest, that scared me a little in that way that demands scrutiny. I held a paper to that spark and watched it flame.

The point is, I found my own curiosity. It helped me back to the page and it helped me crack the carapace of fear that had grown around my heart in effort to protect it. So, today, I wonder, what are you curious about? What has the power to open you, to wake you even just a little bit? Maybe tomorrow morning we can write into the silence together.

A THING I WROTE IN MY JOURNAL

—

Here is an understanding I have of writers:

    We all need support.

    We all need the time to write.

    We all need feedback, even if it's just from one other person.

    We all need to read.

    We all need a vacation.

    We all need to feel valuable or recognized.

    We all need to feel safe.

BEING PRODUCTIVE DOES NOT MEAN
THAT YOU ARE BEING VIRTUOUS

I like to take huge chunks of time off social media. When I do this, it's not about the distraction part, although of course it's better not to have the distraction. Nor is it about the negativity that is often prevalent online. It's more about how I'm using my brain.

There's something about social media that makes me contemplate myself in the wrong way, or at least in a way that is disconnected from the act of writing fiction. My posts are meant to be immediately read, as a reflection of myself, even if they are not *about* me, necessarily. There is a part of my brain that likes to play and have a fun time and entertain people, so it sometimes feels pretty good to participate in that conversation.

But writing fiction (or any kind of long-form project) is a slow burn. It's about writing something that will last, and does not necessarily fill immediate attention needs. I can do both at the same time, tweet and write fiction, and I certainly have. But I write better fiction when I'm not on social media. It's just a fact. And so when I take time off it, it's about creating a boundary for my brain. And thinking, *What kind of writing should I be doing right now?*

It's healthy to contemplate the kinds of writing we're doing and assess how they make us feel, what they accomplish for us, if they move us forward in life, or if we're merely treading water. When I write a tweet, it makes me feel one way; when I write an essay, it makes me feel another way. When I write a newsletter, when I work on my novel, when I work on a television pitch, these give me different feelings, activate different parts of my brain. They can please me, challenge me, help me to progress, all in different ways.

What kinds of things are we writing right now? What do they do for us, how do they open (or close off) our writing? Are we all certain we're using our time wisely? Is the more casual writing worth it? (It certainly can be!) I'm not talking about the distractions here. I'm just talking about contemplating what we get out of everything.

And I don't think there's any sort of moral judgment that needs to happen with this kind of examination. There's no judgment of our core being, because there is no right or wrong answer. We are neither bad nor good people for how we use our writing time. Being productive does not mean we are being virtuous.

But if we're looking to make progress in our work, we should contemplate how we're spending our time, how we're using our beautiful brains.

ALISSA NUTTING

I've come to understand all the different types of work that can go into writing—there's brainstorming, editing, revising, rereading, outlining, researching, engaging in inspiration and influences . . . I definitely don't always feel like *writing* writing, hammering out the original material. And it's true that as a writer I do often have to do *writing* writing when I don't feel like it. And it's true that the more I write whether or not I feel like it, the easier/more familiar that practice gets. But some hours, days, weeks . . . it just isn't possible. Children are screaming and literally clinging to my body, or I'm scheduled for meetings every hour, etc. At those times, instead of not working on my project, I've started asking myself, *What could I manage right now?* Could I tinker with a paragraph? Brainstorm about a scene I'm imagining writing soon? Read a chapter of a book that has an affinity with the book I'm trying to write? If I can't move forward in terms of the manuscript word count on any given day, I'll try to still figure out a way to do something in the service of my project that allows for the circumstances of my life over the next twenty-four hours.

I AM NOT WRITING TODAY

There was a winter recently where there were a few days I couldn't write. I just couldn't. I felt all emptied out. I went for a long walk just so I didn't have to pace my own floors anymore. Something will come out of this walk, I hoped, but all I could think about was *why* I wasn't writing.

By the time I arrived home I realized that my only option was to explore that specifically—the why not. So, I wrote into the not-writing. It turned out it was because I didn't have all the information I needed about a specific topic, but I hadn't seen that yet. I was spinning too hard on the fact that I wasn't getting anything done. I took a step back. I called a friend I needed to interview about a specific moment in time. She remembered details I hadn't. And then I stopped circling and dove into the scene.

"I am not writing because" could be a helpful way to start a sentence if you're having trouble today.

I know for a lot of people the answer can be obvious. Because there are too many people in my house. Because I have too much work to do. Because I'm having health issues. Because I can't find the quiet moments I need to listen to my brain. I hear you, and I send you love and support and the hope that someday you will have the time and space you need to be the fullest version of your writer self. That part of you isn't going anywhere. It will always be waiting for you.

The writer self is waiting for all of us. Take that first step to clear the blocks. Ask yourself why.

LIZ MOORE

I'm going to write about writing while quarantined with two kids under four because
    A. that's my life right now, and
    B. it's the most pressurized form of writing I've ever experienced, and
    C. it might apply to you whether or not you have kids.

    I've always worked full-time, except in grad school, when I worked part-time on top of school. From 2005 to 2016, I learned to balance work and writing, which primarily meant learning to write when tired, and developing the stamina and discipline to stick to a writing routine.

    In 2016, I had my first child. She taught me to balance work, writing, and newborn-induced sleep deprivation.

    In 2019, I had my second child. He taught me to balance work, writing, newborn-induced sleep deprivation, and toddler mood management.

    Then 2020 happened. In 2020, there is no longer "balance." There is only chaos. I published a novel on January 7 and headed out on book tour immediately. No writing occurred. In March, the book tour came to an abrupt halt. My husband and I both continued to work full-time from home, but now we had two kids under four at home with us all. The. Time. For a month, my cold streak with writing continued.

    In April, after several emotional breakdowns in a row,

I resumed writing. It no longer felt like a luxury. Instead, it felt foundational—something situated near the sturdy bottom of Maslow's hierarchy of needs. I missed writing. Specifically, I missed the feeling of accomplishment and self-worth and routine that writing brings me. For me, writing is a shortcut to feeling like myself, remembering who I am and what I hope to bring to the world. It brings me peace and well-being like nothing else does, even when it's going badly, which it is, most of the time. It's simply the act of doing it that calms me.

So recently, I made the decision to use the very few hours I have to myself (typically, one or two per day, sometimes only at nap time) to write. This means that I don't clean, or cook, or do email correspondence, or shop for what we need online, or do taxes, or talk on the phone, or sleep, or mess around on the internet, or anything else. I just write. (The rest of the tasks get done by my husband or by me on weekends, when we can swap off childcare for longer stretches.) Some days go terribly. Some days go better. I'm working on several writing projects at the moment, and I try to rotate them, so on Monday I'll work on project A, on Tuesday I'll work on project B, and on Wednesday I'll work on project C—and so on. This is not ideal, because I can't get completely into the groove with any of them, but I'm inching forward on all of them.

And, most important, the time affords me some brief moments of well-being in the middle of what has otherwise been a very challenging time.

I don't know what lesson to take from this, and I don't know what lesson you'll take from it. It's a weird time. I guess what I've learned is that writing always bobs like a buoy to the surface of my life, no matter what else is going on around me. I'm glad for that.

WRITING THROUGH GRIEF

A few years ago, there was a period in my life when I was thinking about grief. The topic occupied my mind quite a bit. I contemplated how to keep writing when one is grieving—if that's even possible. Writing on top of grief, or I guess *through* grief, seems possible, but difficult. And what about writing *around* grief? Just ignoring it entirely? Well, good luck, friend, with that.

What I finally arrived at is the idea of writing straight *at* grief. To imagine it on one side of the room while the writer is on the other side, and having an approach of meeting it in the middle. To take feelings and attach them to characters, for example. To write in moments for characters to have revelations that we would like to have. To let them execute whatever stage of grief is available to us even if it doesn't have anything to do with the book itself. Just as an exercise. A way to touch work again, or at least the idea of it.

Grief on one side, the writer on the other. And in the middle is a pile of words.

Also, I was thinking about how when it's not destroying us, grief is sometimes comforting. Like a neighborhood street cat who rubs against our ankles in the morning, then digs up our flower beds in the afternoon. Which is to say grief can be familiar to you and thus pleasant in that way. It shows up every day. Grief comes and goes as it pleases. We don't get to choose when we're done with it.

Frustrating, for those of us who work best with schedules. What about those who need to know when and how this feeling will end? What about those of us who have some work to do?

Grief can envelop us as if we are bound by fabric. Eventually we find a way to tear the material. We find a way out, to live again. Perhaps to write again. Even just to breathe first, though, would be good.

When we are ready to let it go, we will let it go and not a second sooner. It might be when we least expect it. But I leave this here as a placeholder for when you arrive at that moment, if any of us need it.

When you get there, let it go. And then write.

LAILA LALAMI

For years my writing process was so boring that I felt embarrassed whenever I was asked about it. First, I divided my weekly schedule into teaching and nonteaching days. (Teaching requires all my attention and emotion and, while I might get an idea for a scene or come up with an interesting bit of dialogue, I tend to save all those stray thoughts for when I'm not teaching.) Then, to get through a first draft, I wrote five hundred words a day on my nonteaching days. Once a draft is complete, I stopped aiming for a specific word count and went wherever revision took me. It was a simple enough process, and it worked.

Then the pandemic happened.

I had two books scheduled to be launched (the paperback of my novel *The Other Americans* in March 2020, and the hardcover of my essay collection *Conditional Citizens* in April 2020). All my plans for them fell through. Just work on your next one, my agent advised. But I couldn't. I mean, the world was falling apart around me! In June, I got sick and had to have surgery. In September, my dad died. I fell into a deep depression.

At some point a few months later, I went into my office

and just stared out the window. I felt as if I would never write another book. Then I got to thinking about a book idea I'd had back in 2014, a wild premise that I felt I would never be able to execute. I pulled out the document and read it purely as a distraction. I could see why the story, as I'd conceived it then, wouldn't work, but there were parts of it that did work. As I said, it was a distraction. I wrote a couple of sentences that day. The next, I think I deleted one of those and wrote another one. That was all I could manage.

I found so much relief in this distraction that I made a deal with myself. Instead of worrying about word counts, I would commit to spending two hours at my desk. Those two hours became a respite from my depression, the mounting death toll, the terrible state of the world—all the things I couldn't control. It took months of this practice before the distraction became an obsession, and eventually a novel.

Be gentle with yourself, is what I'm trying to say. If schedules and rules work for you, then write up schedules and make up rules. If collecting ideas and taking notes until you're ready works for you, then do that. Find what works. Then be ready to change it if it doesn't work any longer.

WRITE FOR THOSE WHO CANNOT

I don't mean to sound like someone's mother telling them to clean their plate at dinner because there are children starving in the world, but there are people who don't have access to the technology you have, who can't afford books or notebooks, who are denied an education and may never even learn how to read or write. Not to mention people who genuinely do not have the time to write because they need to work multiple jobs just to survive and support their family. Or who have health issues or disabilities that might prevent them from writing. People who don't have the same freedom of speech as you because of their political situations and are terrified to write. People who are unfairly imprisoned and are denied peace and safety and quiet, let alone the beautiful pen that quivers at all our fingertips. People who have been made to shut up their entire lives.

You should write 1000 words for yourself because you *can*, and you should write 1000 words for those who cannot.

MEGAN MAYHEW-BERGMAN

I sold my novel just after my first collection of stories came out. A lot of things happened to me in those years that followed, but two fundamental things were true:

1. I didn't yet know what raw ingredients I would most need to sustain a novel I wanted to stand behind, so I had to learn by trying and failing. I didn't want to write an adequate book; I wanted to write a good book. My first versions felt adequate, not outstanding.

2. I had roughly three crises in between selling my book and publishing an entirely different one. I believe in the power of the personal crisis—but it also remakes you as a person. Your sensibilities and humanity might change. Mine did. A different person has to write a different book—so draft upon draft happened. And was trashed. And restarted. I read more. I suffered more. The world changed rapidly. My children aged. I grew. As I reversioned as a human, so did my work. Sometimes this meant the project I started was no longer the project I wanted to finish.

I knew the early drafts weren't right when I didn't want to press them into people's hands. I feel proud of the last version—it feels textured and cohesive, provocative. For me, when I imagined sharing earlier versions with people I respected, I got a knot in my stomach. I did get frustrated with how long it was taking me to get the book right—I had to recommit to creativity and art, and detach myself from commercial outcomes. When I did that, I was able to realize that the book wasn't going to be conventional, and that suddenly became okay, and then more than okay—it felt exciting. That's when I knew.

It took me several full drafts and restarts to finally make a book that felt the way I wanted this book to feel, which is, weirdly, now a short novel and a handful of short stories. And somehow it is more right than anything I began with.

REBECCA MAKKAI

I've been teaching an advanced novel-writing workshop in
Chicago for eleven years now, twelve writers in each one.
That's 132 first-time novelists who spend one year with me
out of the many it will take them to finish this book. One
of the first things I tell them is that my first novel took me
ten years to complete—not because I was working full-time
(I was) or because I had two babies in that time (I did) but
because I would occasionally lose faith in the project. And
because ten years is such a long time that I, and my interests
and my tastes and my skill level, changed many times, and
the book had to keep up.

What I've seen is that every single novelist I've ever
taught loses hold of their book at some point, or at many
points. The important thing to understand is that when you
lose your book, it's not because it's a flawed book or somehow the *wrong* book but because no one can sustain contin-
uous ardor for anything (or anyone) for several years. It's still
your book.

The following are not reasons to give up on it: You're
mad at it, it needs tearing apart and putting back together,
you get scared of failure, you get scared of success, you can't

stand your own voice, the whole thing is ridiculous, someone didn't like the part they read, you're supposed to have a real job, you can't remember what you're doing, this thing is a mess. Here is the only reason to give up on it: For a sustained period of time (several months) you have absolutely no feeling toward it whatsoever. Even then, don't delete the file. You never know.

GIVING CRITICISM

It's a challenge to be a good first reader of a book. We have to react to what we're critiquing not just as a reader but also as a fellow writer, as part of a bigger community. We have to draw on wells of generosity, because we have to be present on many pages of something that is inherently imperfect, and that is a long haul to be paying that kind of attention to something that isn't quite right yet. And we have to shut off our egos, the arguments in our heads, about how we would do it if we were writing it ourselves. This is not for us to put our mark on: this isn't our book, it's theirs.

My friend the Canadian writer Claire Cameron is an ideal first reader for me. She reads my work quickly, and then sends me thoughtful emails about big picture things. Nothing too picky, because those kinds of comments can frustrate a writer, especially when they are in the most vulnerable state as the first-draft state. And she doesn't give me intense line edits, because I suspect she knows that's not her job; there's a copy editor coming along in the future, and they'll have me pushing words and commas around the page soon enough.

She wrestles instead with structure and themes. I always sense she thinks about what she has to say, but also what she thinks I would be interested in hearing. She always tries to help me write my book, in my voice, in my way.

It can be tricky. Sometimes we see our friends' blind spots, glaring and blinking at us. They have asked for our honest opinion, and now we have to figure out how to give it. Can we do it gently? Can we do it with grace?

I like to read 'em like Claire does, all in one go. I love to spend a weekend with a friend's book and inhale it and then give them my instant response in an email. I don't like to send more than an email. Sometimes I make notes in the Word document, because it's easier for me to keep track of things that way, but at this point, I would never send it to an author unless they asked for it first.

A lot of authors will ask you what kind of notes you want from them, and it can also be helpful if you are clear and tell them yourself. For my seventh novel, which was set in New Orleans, I had several readers who were born and raised in this town, and all I wanted from them was feedback on how I wrote about the city. I have certain readers who I can count on for their commercial sensibility. I have some readers who are structure nerds, like I am. Each book requires different kinds of reads. I try to be smart and strategic and respectful—I don't want to waste anyone's time, and I don't want to ask someone to read a book that they would absolutely hate. This is a huge favor I'm asking.

I've also had first readers I didn't click with, for whatever reason. (No indictments here. It's nice that people cared to try and offered their time.) And I'm sure I have given less than helpful reads. I've had to grow in so many ways. Nearly everything I write about with confidence comes out of learning from the mistakes I made first. One crucial thing I have learned, which I mentioned above: I have to remember when giving notes, this is not my book, this is theirs. And the other most crucial thing is this: Being a first reader is an actual gift we can give someone—it can change the life of a book—and so, we must do it with care. This is a way we build our writing community. This is a way we look out for each other.

RECEIVING CRITICISM

How do you know when you're ready to ask for criticism? And how do you properly receive it?

I have different stages of asking for feedback. I usually send something out to a few trusted readers when I have about one hundred pages or so to see if there's anything interesting or worthy happening in what I'm working on. What I want to know is if I'm heading on the right path or not. Sometimes I'll send a chapter or two to a friend here and there just to see if it makes them laugh or feels fun or affecting. And then there are various stages of doneness. Done with a complete first draft does not necessarily mean it's fit for consumption yet. I tend to send out a second or third draft to my agent for feedback. I don't like to ask people to read multiple drafts of my work if I can help it. By the time I get to the place where I can send it to my editor, it needs to be in top shape. Her comments are the ones that will take me across the finish line.

Once I spent three days in the woods in Mississippi with my dog and a big pile of notes from my editor. During the day I made my way through pine cones and spiderwebs and sharp cuts of huge chunks of text. It was sunny and seventy and I ate a lot of potato chips. At night it got chilly, so I built a fire and got dreamy and let my mind wander. There was no internet in my cabin but if I walked up to the main road, I could get service on my phone. The news remained no good—I didn't want to see what was going on in the world—but I wanted to post pictures of the woods on Instagram so people would know I was still alive.

I thought long and hard about the notes my editor gave me. It was my fifth book with her. She's one of the best in the business and, beyond that, knows my strengths and weaknesses intimately. Her thoughts are worth gold. As I read her notes, I had, at times, to put my ego by the wayside. We are constantly being asked as writers to put our egos by the wayside, even as we must channel them to give us the courage and energy to get us through the writing process in the first place. What a wild emotional ride it is to be an artist sometimes.

But I called on the approach I've always used in the past—not just with her but with other people's critiques of my work—that has worked best for me. Because her thoughts and my work deserved to be treated with a positive attitude.

1. **Don't freak out.** No matter what, I usually get a little zing in my heart when I read through someone else's comments on my work. This could be an editor or a peer or my agent or whoever. Someone else is reacting to my writing, and thus I have a reaction to that in return. But I tell myself nothing is permanent, these are honest responses from someone you trust, and whatever is wrong can be fixed—if it really does need fixing. I'm also not required to agree with everything they say. But I must, at the very least, listen calmly, because I'm the one who has asked their opinion.

2. **Read it straight through.** I like to sit down and do a steady read of all my editor's notes and consume it all at once, just set aside as much time as I will need to hear her voice in my head. I want to know all the issues at the same time, carry them all with me in my head, just as I've been carrying the book in me for so long. I want to understand the scale of it, the entire universe of the book, and where the holes are within it. It makes me feel like a hundred tiny flames are lighting at once within me. This helps me to respond in a holistic way. Everything has to connect in our books. It all has to hold together.

3. **Contend with the cuts.** In the end my editor cut five chapters out of twenty-two of that book. Big meaty chunks of

text tossed into the fireplace. In my mind I watched them burn. And then I said to myself: Can I view the cuts as an opportunity? Can I recognize that sometimes I write things only to arrive at other places in my work? Can I see that the words are being cleared to make way for better words? So much of my writing is about pacing and creating a speedy, rhythmic reading experience; I didn't want anything getting in the way of that. A few of the chapters, I didn't blink at their removal, and I didn't miss them when they were gone. With a few of the others, I resurrected some of the material and placed it in other chapters. One brand-new chapter was spawned from the wreckage. Sometimes things just don't work and never will, and sometimes things don't work yet, and you can improve on them until they do. The point is not to be resentful of this experience but to acknowledge that this is simply a chance to make the work better.

While I was in the woods, I didn't change too much of the document. I brainstormed instead. I sat quietly by a creek as the fall leaves scattered around me and I closed my eyes and listened. I thought of the big overarching issues of the book and how I might solve them. The only thing I can do is take it step-by-step. There is no rushing through this process. Some days during editing I'll only make it through a few pages, and other days I'll skip through a few chapters at once. I have to wrestle with it, refine it, bend it into shape. I can set goals, make schedules, but ultimately edits take as long as they're going to take. All any of us can do is listen to the words.

MEG WOLITZER

One of the things that can happen when you're writing a novel is that you forget how excited you were in the very beginning, when everything seemed possible. You lose that initial flush of love, and all the writing prompts in the world won't always bring it back. Sometimes you can sort of back into that feeling not through your own work but through someone else's. What I try to do when bleakness and indifference descend is to find a passage in someone else's fiction—in a book I have loved—that I feel sure the writer was excited about when he or she wrote it. Exciting and excited fiction can itself excite you. Then you watch the flames jump from that book to yours, and it just might be enough.

WRITE IT DOWN, PUT IT AWAY

Once I was upset with someone. I couldn't shake it. I hadn't spoken to them in a year. Finally, I wrote an email to them. I didn't send it. I just wrote it. I rewrote it a few times. I still didn't send it. I thought about what it would mean if I did send it. If I would feel any better or worse if they knew how I felt—how I still felt a year later. I didn't know what it would accomplish. It was enough that I had written it down, I felt. They didn't need to hear it coming from me. I felt better having written it, though. That seemed like enough.

Lest you think I have arrived at some higher emotional plane than the rest of the planet, months later I did take a line from the email and put it in a character's mouth. Come on—it was a really good email! But mostly the words remained between me, myself, and I.

A place to put my feelings, the written word. A place to feel secure.

ANOTHER THING I WROTE IN MY JOURNAL

I know you are worried this book is a mess, but you just have to finish this first draft and then you can fix it. The holes are glaring at you already, but you can't fix air, you can't fix nothingness. Just write these chapters already.

Do not lose faith or heart. Write these stories.

There is still time to get everything done.

MYCHAL DENZEL SMITH

I am extremely lucky in that I have practically all the time in the world to write. I don't have any other job besides writing. I'm not saying this to brag but to hold myself accountable for the fact that I have nothing to do but write and still somehow manage to be late with every first draft. I like to think editors enjoy working with me, but I temper that with the knowledge that every single editor, whether they say it or not, is a little peeved at me for the number of extensions I request in getting that initial draft to their inbox. It's just a first draft.

Except I have never been able to think of a first draft as just a first draft. I am ten years into my writing career (and feeling every ache of it) and still stress over first drafts as though they will go straight to print.

Part of this is a result of starting my writing career in the internet era. There is very little editing that goes into the work that goes online. Sure, at some of our more august publications, with money and copy editors and fact-checkers to spare, there's a fairly rigorous process. But I didn't start out writing for those places. I began my career writing for online publications that needed content, lots of it, as quickly as possible. Little care is given to craft in this situation.

But I can't blame it all on the culture and economics of the internet. I am slow. I write very slowly. I write first drafts at a pace that frustrates and infuriates. I spend weeks not writing at all. I'm a bit lazy, and it's much easier to do nothing than to agonize over words and ideas. The Golden Age of Television will not watch itself (though maybe, at some point, it will?). Still, that's not the reason I am on the couch, laptop open, blank page staring back at me. It's because I'm scared.

If you're reading this, I assume you're a writer and you're familiar with how intimidating the blank page can be. On its own, it's frightening. But I have also come to believe that I can't ever make a mistake, that I must turn in perfect, ready-to-print first drafts, or else I will never be able to write again. There are a number of reasons for this, and I'll save the act of enumerating them for my therapist. For now, I'll simply say that this idea, which grows with each new work, holds me in a cycle of self-hatred and self-pulverizing.

I have, as stated, been writing professionally for ten years. I cannot survive another ten years being this unkind to myself. But I never thought I would make it this far. I have written this way because I have genuinely believed that each piece would be my last. I have not believed in redemption.

It's only now, two books in and preparing to teach writing in earnest, that I'm coming to believe there is more to my career than a single moment, a knockout essay to end all essays, a calling card. I have built a body of work; I am building a body of work. You are building a body of work. The first draft is never the last draft—it isn't even the first draft anymore. You approach each blank page with the experience and wisdom of the previous blank pages that you've conquered. You will do something new with this one, but it is not something you're unprepared for. Everything you've done has led you to this moment. And you will get some of it wrong. Then you will revise until it is right. And you'll keep building your body of work.

I am learning now to let go, to believe I am worthy of a messy draft because I am worthy of a career that is not defined by one book, one essay, one paragraph, one sentence. You are. We are.

BEGINNING AGAIN

A book is just a pile of words that you have accumulated over a period of time. There is some strategy along the way and of course there is intention, heart, soul behind it. But when we sit down every day, to write, for a long time it's just one giant heap of words. That's how every book starts. There is no way around it. The way we make the pile is that we show up every day and we build it. We show up for our art and we show up for this imaginary universe that somehow exists in our mind and is then transferred to the page. And then at the end of this journey, six months, a year, two years, we start over again, we look at our work in a new way, from a new angle, and we revise. We do this again and again until it's done. So, when we talk about finishing the first draft, I'm sorry to say it's not the ending. Because the second draft is a new beginning. But I don't mind it. This universe we have created is asking for justice, for its due. We begin again until we are done.

THE RELEASE

Sometimes we're afraid to let things go because letting go means moving forward. Sometimes finishing something means you'll never get that time back in your life, and that feels significant to you, maybe makes you feel uncomfortable or sad or scared. Sometimes finishing a project means you'll finally have to show your work to people, to make yourself vulnerable to the world. Sometimes it feels good to obsess over things, to revise the same words over and over again. I know that feeling. I've finally figured everything out with this book, I think. Can't I just stay in this place forever?

If you don't let it go, you'll never know if it's any good. If you don't let it go, no one will ever hear what you have to say. If you don't let it go, you'll never find out what happens next. If you don't let it go, then you'll be stuck here forever.

JOSH GONDELMAN

I always joke to my brilliant wife, Maris, that I am the King of "Good Enough." I'm an absolute expert at barfing out fast, sloppy, that's-fine-for-now first-draft copy. In the long run, my occasional proclivity toward leaving serviceable but not quite right prose on the page occasionally bites me in the ass. But far more often, my keyboard mashing is an asset. It sends my work in the generally right direction, or it lets me know—on rereading—that I'm off in the wilderness and need to reorient. And no one ever has to know the content of your hasty scribbles. What happens in first drafts stays in first drafts . . . unless it's worth saving for a final version. It's far more useful to have a big pile of maybe than the hypothetical perfect arrangement of sentences that you're certain you'll eventually shake out of your head if you just pound it long enough like a Heinz ketchup bottle. All that is to say, I encourage you to embrace your inner Good Enough.

THE FIRST DRAFT WILL BE FLAWED

No matter how prepared you are, the first draft will still turn out to be imperfect. Know that going into this process. A common holdup for writers is wanting to make their first draft flawless, when the reality is all books are at least a little imperfect until they get through the copyediting stage. I admire those who can spit out a refined first draft. As for me, I count on my second or third draft to really sing. My first draft is the place where I dump the raw material. But the good news is it's also where a lot of honest feelings and original ideas show up, too.

You already have some of those words in your head, fluttering about in a gentle whirlwind, just waiting to be put in some kind of order. Picture them in a summer storm, the kind that blows in and litters blossoms everywhere, leaving behind a damp and rich earth. See the words for what they are: electricity all around you. You want them organized and tidy and neat, and I want that, too. But love those words for just being words, too—and see what comes out of it. And then build on those flaws.

I let a draft sit for a while when I'm done with it. A few weeks maybe, no more than that. I don't like to take too much time away. Still, I read, I catch up on whatever emails I left unattended because I was deep in the throes of finishing this draft. I stretch, I walk. I give myself a little forgiveness before I read what I have written, because I know there will be (many) mistakes in it. But there will be surprises, too. Real emotional moments. This draft will be flawed, I tell myself. But it's the beginning of something good. And then I dive in again.

DANTIEL MONIZ

I'm going to be really honest—I didn't write a single new thing, a thing that was for me, all of 2020. I had just finished a stint as a visiting writer the December before, I was in the middle of revising my forthcoming collection with my editor, and I was thinking a lot about where the money might come from next. I had what I told myself were valid excuses. But I had two writing residencies coming up, one in the spring and one in the fall, and it was fine. The work—the will to work— would come back. I wasn't writing but I was still a writer, right? It was March, and in a couple of days, I would embark for San Antonio with dear friends I hadn't seen in at least a year and that would jump-start it all, surely. And then, well, we all know what happened next. Between the pandemic, protests, and the presidential election, the not-writing folded over and consumed me. And mostly, what I felt was shame. I thought, what if this is it? What if I never write again? All this expectancy people have for me, wasted.

I think about how I might have been better able to mitigate those fears if our artmaking wasn't so entwined with a capitalist kind of productivity. With this drive for the next book and the next book and the next book without real consideration for the time it takes to produce art or the distinctiveness of our individual processes or that sometimes the world simply requires one to witness. The fallow periods and daydreaming and TV-watching. The energy it takes to care for and nourish our bodies (especially this; how easy to forget we are animal, and we need). All things that are essential to writing but aren't classified as writing. Actions and inactions necessary to refill the well.

Thankfully, I have a strong community of friends that reminded me to allow myself grace, and I was able to begin the process of shedding that shame. To sit with myself and distinguish between my own internality and an external pressure I'd somehow allowed to slip inside. And after I could identify where the fear was coming from, after I acknowledged and released it, I felt excitement and relief. I could feel the words burbling inside that quiet place in my mind that draws me to language and stories in the first place. It was always there.

If any of this feels familiar, I'm telling you the way I was told—extend yourself grace. You're okay. Whether it's been a few days since you last touched the work or a few years, it's yours and it's there whenever you're ready. Remember you like this; that you're called to it. Take a deep breath. Hold it for five seconds. And release. Okay. Let's get back to the page.

DONE IS BETTER THAN PERFECT

I have a friend, a woman, who lives out west, who has been working on a project for a long time, years and years. She is a craftsman, an artist, and she is extremely focused on getting things right. The project is long overdue, but she continues to push past the deadline, obsessively trying to perfect it. I admire her talent and commitment so much.

She lives in the desert, about twenty minutes from town, and every day, early in the morning, she hops in her truck and goes to a café and sees the same people she has seen for the past few years. And they talk about their families and their lives for a while. She pets other people's dogs, she watches their children get older, comments on how tall they've gotten. She stays for a few hours, lingering, because she knows when she goes home, it's back to work.

This summer we talked for a while about everything, the work she'd done, the work she still needed to do. I noted her ever-shifting deadline. She admitted that working on this project for so long has gotten in the way of some of her relationships and has also prevented her from moving on in her life. I said to her gently, "You know sometimes done is better than perfect."

What she's making is incredible—I've seen parts of it—but also it's already incredible; she's consistently operating on a high level. All she has to do is finish it now, but (I think) finishing it would mean that she's done and then she would have to figure out what she has to do next. And I also suspect she takes comfort in what she's doing as much as it tortures her to still be working on this damn project after all this time. When it feels so good, when it's humming, you never want to be done.

Still, I believe done is better than perfect. And there is even a kind of perfection to just being done in the first place. A perfection in completeness. It's not that I don't think we should strive for greatness—I always shoot for the stars. But I think finishing things is crucially important. And I don't believe that anything can ever be perfect. I have never written a "perfect" book in my life, and it's a fool's errand to try.

Someday when my friend finishes her project and it's out in the world—and she will, I know she will, I believe in her—I promise you she will point out its flaws to me in a low voice. And I will say "I never would have noticed." Because I would have been too busy admiring what was great about it.

And there's always going to be one tiny thing wrong. That tiny imperfection is the thing that we can sometimes love most in the end.

7

ALL YEAR ROUND

Creativity happens all the time, whether we know it or not. We just have to learn to pay attention to it. And we can be at any stage of the creative process all year round. We can always be thinking and observing and consuming and processing, even if there's no visible output. You can also just exist in your life, too, and that is wonderful. You don't need to be consistently viewing the world through an artistic lens. But I just want you to know that this creative side of yourself is always available to access in one way or another. One thousand words is a beautiful guideline. But you are the ultimate creator of your guidelines. You drive your future creativity. You don't need me or this book or anyone to tell you how to make your art. It's year-round, this work, this life. What you can count on is yourself, sitting down and doing that work. And the relationships you build along the way.

At any moment we can be in any place with our work. How do we ground ourselves during those times? I return to the same questions over and over again. What kind of writer do I want to be? What kind of story do I want to tell? How do I make space for my writing? Where do I sit? How do I get out of my own way? How do I stop judging my own writing? How do I embrace the joy of making a mess with my work? How can I write without fear? How can I commit to myself? How can I show up consistently for myself? And how can I forgive myself for that which I have simply not done yet?

And I return to the same strategies. I do this in pursuit of stability, creativity, and community. I do this in pursuit of art. I invite you to join me. All year round.

PATRICIA LOCKWOOD

I will tell a story that began in summer 2021. One afternoon—
July 11, to be precise—I drank a cup of mushroom tea, swam,
listened to music in the sunlight, thought, then fell asleep for
a very long time. I woke the next morning, walked automatically to my rock-and-pebble collection, and began pulling out
stones. Amazonite, jasper, green garnet, rainbow obsidian, gold
rutile. The names came to my lips as if they had been waiting,
faster than I could write them down. The Lock, the Door, the
Key. The Exchange, the Wand, the Insect. Ghost on the Slopes,
a phantom quartz. Tooth and Claw, the Fingerprint. Waves
in the World, or the Pattern. Poetry, or the Flash of Meaning.
Cave of the Winds, a Fairburn agate—when I first picked it
up, I seemed to see a woman sitting cross-legged inside, brown
hair streaming over her shoulders.

    The Stones, I would call them. A system, like tarot. A
planchette like James Merrill used, his long billionaire fingers
floating over the board. I'd draw a spread every morning,
three stones, five stones, seven. Sometimes they would read
my life, but just as often they would read what I was working on. If I drew the Camera, it meant to look outward. If I
drew the Rosy Heart it meant to have hope, be tender; and
if I drew the Runes it meant to consider the whole. If I drew
the Insect (a scorpion set in a resin ball, that came from God

knows where) it would mean I was in a cycle of obsession, revising the same sentence over and over. But if I drew the Fairburn agate, I would see something more: a whole book in the air that I ought to be writing. Immediately after the entry listing all the stones and their meanings, there are the first notes for a novel about a girl sitting cross-legged inside a cave, brown hair streaming over her shoulders.

The Stones went in a white linen pouch—scalloped, embroidered, smelling of candle wax. I think it must have been French, from the 1910s or 1920s, one of those little bags called *aumônières* for Catholic girls to carry to church. For a while I carried them everywhere: on planes, in my backpack, feeling incomplete when I left them at home—the way you do when you leave your notebook in the white-hot middle of writing something. What was within was so active, alive as a keyboard; interacted with my body like a body. I reached in and consulted them almost every day for a year, and then after a long while whole weeks went by, and recently the Stones have sat in my top drawer for months. I'm not sure why. Did their season come to an end? Did they no longer need me to make meaning, did I no longer need them to find it? I had put aside the novel they had first helped me conceptualize, the protagonist in the cave with her long brown hair, sure that it was beyond my strength. I worked on other things that seemed more within reach: no amethyst, no sunstone, no pearls. But I took them out again to write this, looked into the Cave, and saw her again, sitting cross-legged, sending her thin voice up toward a hole in the ceiling. Maybe they waited. Maybe they *were* the novel, set aside for a spell. But sometimes something has to be lost, or churned underground for a while, to be given the chance to turn up again.

YOU CAN DO IT

The year I'm writing this book is the year where a lot of us started to come out of something and see people again. I flew to foreign countries to speak to beautiful strangers in bookstores and I visited some of my favorite city literary festivals in America. The last trip of the year I took was to Austin, to their wonderful Texas Book Festival, and I met so many new people, I shook hands, I talked all day about my projects, but also everyone else's projects, too, all the people who wrote, who identified as writers, or who were readers, or who were teachers, and we were all together, and were happy to meet each other.

At night, after the hours of meeting and talking, there was a party, and I walked to it from my hotel, through the streets of Austin, just sort of ambling along slowly, thinking about how tired I was, not just from the excitement of the day but also how I had written so many words already that year, in my life. I thought about that well, the one we all have to tend to within ourselves, the one that sometimes needs filling. But then I thought about all the positive energy I had received that day and how I immediately wanted to turn it back around again, turn it into something, return it to people if I could, too. I just heard these words in my head: *You can do it.* The most obvious of phrases but when we have been working and fighting and trying to stay inspired for a long time, what other words will suffice?

It became a bit of a chant in my head. You can do it, you can do it, you can do it.

Whatever it is you're working on, whatever it is you're dreaming about, whatever path you're trying to carve out for yourself, whatever electricity you're trying to generate, whatever voice you're trying to draw out of yourself, whatever way you're trying to connect with people, whatever you're trying to communicate with the world, whatever fire you are trying to start this morning today this week forever and ever, you can fucking do it.

One thousand words, all year round. You can do it.

HOW DO YOU KNOW WHEN YOU'RE DONE?

I think so much about endings. When things will be over. When we can move on to whatever comes next. I think about it in terms of the world, this country, the health and success and stability of people in my life. And because I'm always working on one thing or another, I think about it in terms of books.

How do you know when a book is done? It took me a few novels to figure out how to answer that question, at least in terms of fiction.

As someone who writes character-driven fiction, I like to go around to all my characters and check in with them, ask them if they have anything else to say, if there's anything else they want to add to the conversation. Plot so often exists for me as a place to hang the growth of a character. So I need to know: Did I take your story as far as it could go? Did you get to where you needed to be in this book? And they'll tell me.

In terms of memoir, I asked myself two questions.

The first was: Is there anything left I'm willing to share? Because there's no way I can cover my entire life, and I'm not going to spill all my secrets. That's not why I wrote a memoir. Of course, this is a personal and nuanced question. I'm the only one who knows my boundaries.

And secondly, have all the themes come to fruition? I made lists of the overarching themes and tracked their progress through the book. When each one finally got a check mark next to them, I felt done.

I have also always shared my work with peers and my editor because they can offer insight on the doneness of a project.

Trust your advisors, access your resources. They're in your life because they're smart. I ask friends for their opinions all the time. *Did this chapter take you somewhere? Do you see any holes? Did I land this plane?*

Of course, you can only trust yourself most of all. You know how far you want and need to take your work.

And of course, there's your gut. But first we must learn to even listen to our guts in the first place, how to trust ourselves. How to ask the right questions. Like: Do you feel like you're done writing this book? Have you given it your all? Have you scraped inside every crevice of your soul? Sit with yourself. Look around in there. Is there anything left to tell?

No one knows your answers but you. Are you prepared to ask the questions?

THE END GOAL

The end goal isn't selling a book and making a million dollars and hitting the bestseller list, although I would never say no to any of those things. The end goal is putting the words on the page and finishing what you started. And what you can build from that.

CHOOSE TO WRITE

You have the choice between the empty page and the full page. A choice to build something out of thin air. Choose fullness. Choose a sense of completeness. An abundance of words, yours if you want. A thing you can do for yourself, for free, today, now. Choose to write.

ABOUT THE CONTRIBUTORS

Megan Abbott is the Edgar Award–winning author of ten crime novels, including *You Will Know Me*, *Give Me Your Hand*, and the *New York Times* bestseller *The Turnout*. She also writes for television, including *Dare Me*, the series she adapted from her own novel, now streaming on Netflix. Her latest novel is *Beware the Woman* (2023).

Rumaan Alam is the author of the novels *Rich and Pretty*, *That Kind of Mother*, and *Leave the World Behind*.

Kristen Arnett is the queer author of *With Teeth: A Novel* (Riverhead Books, 2021), which was a finalist for the Lambda Literary Award in fiction, and the *New York Times* bestselling debut novel *Mostly Dead Things* (Tin House, 2019), which was short-listed for the VCU Cabell First Novelist Award.

Born and raised in Florida, **Laura van den Berg** is the author of five works of fiction, including *The Third Hotel*, a finalist for the New York Public Library Young Lions Fiction Award, and *I Hold a Wolf by the Ears*, one of *Time* magazine's 10 Best Fiction Books of 2020. She is the recent recipient of a Guggenheim Fellowship, a Strauss Livings Award from the American Academy of Arts and Letters, and a literature fellowship from the National Endowment for the Arts. Her next novel, *Florida Diary*, is forthcoming from FSG.

Rebecca Carroll is a writer, cultural critic, and host of the podcasts *Come Through with Rebecca Carroll: Fifteen Essential Conversations* *about Race in a Pivotal Year for America* (WNYC Studios) and *Billie Was a Black Woman* (an Audible original). Rebecca is also the creator and curator of the live event and audio series *In Love and Struggle*, which shares the lives and experiences of Black women in America through monologues, stories, music, and humor. A former critic-at-large for the *Los Angeles Times*, and cultural critic for WNYC/New York Public Radio, Rebecca's writing has been published widely. She is the author of several books about race in America, including the award-winning *Sugar in the Raw: Voices of Young Black Girls in America*, and most recently, her critically acclaimed memoir, *Surviving the White Gaze*. Rebecca is currently editor at large for The Meteor media collective. She lives in Brooklyn with her husband and son.

Alexander Chee is most recently the author of the essay collection *How to Write an Autobiographical Novel*. He teaches creative writing at Dartmouth College and lives in Vermont.

Camille T. Dungy is the author of *Soil: The Story of a Black Mother's Garden*. She has also written *Guidebook to Relative Strangers: Journeys into Race, Motherhood, and History*, a finalist for the National Book Critics Circle Award, and four collections of poetry, including *Trophic Cascade*, winner of the Colorado Book Award. Dungy edited *Black Nature: Four Centuries of African American Nature Poetry*, coedited the *From the Fishouse* poetry anthology, and served as assistant editor for *Gathering Ground: A Reader Celebrating Cave Canem's First Decade*. You may know her as the host of *Immaterial*, a podcast from the Metropolitan Museum of Art and Magnificent Noise. A University Distinguished Professor at Colorado State University, Dungy's honors include the 2021 Academy of American Poets Fellowship, a 2019 Guggenheim Fellowship, an American Book Award, and fellowships from the NEA in both prose and poetry.

Melissa Febos is the bestselling author of four books, most recently *Girlhood*, winner of the National Book Critics Circle Award in criticism, and *Body Work: The Radical Power of Personal Narrative*. She is the recipient of awards and fellowships from the Guggenheim Foundation, the National Endowment for the Arts, MacDowell, Lambda Literary, the Black Mountain Institute, the Barbara Deming Foundation, the British Library, the Bogliasco Foundation, and others. She is an associate professor at the University of Iowa.

Isaac Fitzgerald is the *New York Times* bestselling author of *Dirtbag, Massachusetts* (winner of a New England Book Award). He appears frequently on the *Today* show and is also the author of the bestselling children's book *How to Be a Pirate* as well as the coauthor of *Pen & Ink: Tattoos and the Stories Behind Them* and *Knives & Ink: Chefs and the Stories Behind Their Tattoos* (winner of an IACP Award). His writing has appeared in the *New York Times*, the *Atlantic, Esquire*, the *Guardian, The Best American Nonrequired Reading*, and numerous other publications. He lives in Brooklyn and is currently working on his next book, *American Dionysus*, forthcoming from Knopf.

Roxane Gay's writing appears in *The Best American Nonrequired Reading 2018, The Best American Mystery Stories 2014, The Best American Short Stories 2012, Best Sex Writing 2012, Harper's Bazaar, A Public Space, McSweeney's, Tin House, Oxford American, American Short Fiction, Virginia Quarterly Review*, and many others. She is a contributing opinion writer for the *New York Times*, where she also writes the Work Friend column. She is the author of the books *Ayiti, An Untamed State*, the *New York Times* bestselling *Bad Feminist*, the nationally bestselling *Difficult Women*, and the *New York Times* bestselling *Hunger: A Memoir of My Body*. She is also the author of the Eisner Award–winning *World of Wakanda* for Marvel and the editor of *The Best American Short Stories 2018*. She is currently at work on film and television projects, a book of writing advice, an essay collection about television and culture, and a YA novel entitled *The Year I Learned Everything*. In 2018, she won a Guggenheim Fellowship. She has a newsletter, *The Audacity*. She is also the Gloria Steinem Endowed Chair in Media, Culture, and Feminist Studies at Rutgers University–New Brunswick.

Megan Giddings is an assistant professor at the University of Minnesota. Her first novel, *Lakewood*, was one of *New York* magazine's top ten books of 2020, an NPR Best Book of 2020, a Michigan Notable Book for 2021, a finalist for two NAACP Image Awards, and was a finalist for an L.A. Times Book Prize in the Ray Bradbury Science Fiction, Fantasy, and Speculative Fiction category. Megan's writing has received funding and support from the Barbara Deming Foundation and Hedgebrook. She lives in the Midwest.

Josh Gondelman most recently worked as the head writer and an executive producer for *Desus & Mero* on Showtime. Previously, he spent five years at *Last Week Tonight with John Oliver*, where he earned four Emmy Awards, two Peabody Awards, and three WGA Awards. Josh made his late-night stand-up debut on *Conan* (TBS), and he has also performed on *Late Night with Seth Meyers* (NBC) and *The Late Late Show with James Corden* (CBS). Gondelman is also the author of the essay collection *Nice Try: Stories of Best Intentions and Mixed Results*, published September 2019 by Harper Perennial. Gondelman is the co-author (along with Joe Berkowitz) of the book *You Blew It*, published in 2015 by Plume. In the past, Gondelman wrote for Fuse TV's *Billy on the Street*. His writing has also appeared in publications including *McSweeney's Internet Tendency*, *New York* magazine, and the *New Yorker*.

Christopher Gonzalez is the author of *I'm Not Hungry but I Could Eat* (SFWP 2021). A recipient of the 2021 NYFA/NYSCA Artist

Fellowship in Fiction, his writing appears in *Astra Magazine, Poets &*
Writers online, the *Nation, Catapult, Best Microfictions,* and *Best Small*
Fictions, among other journals and anthologies. He currently lives in
Brooklyn, NY.

Andrew Sean Greer is the author of seven works of fiction, including
The Confessions of Max Tivoli and *Less,* the winner of the 2018 Pulitzer Prize for Fiction. His latest novel is *Less Is Lost.*

Lauren Groff is a three-time National Book Award finalist and the
New York Times bestselling author of the novels *The Monsters of Tem-*
pleton, Arcadia, Fates and Furies, and *Matrix,* and the celebrated short
story collections *Delicate Edible Birds* and *Florida.* She has won the
Story Prize and the PEN/O. Henry Award, and has been a finalist for
the National Book Critics Circle Award. Her work regularly appears
in the *New Yorker,* the *Atlantic,* and elsewhere.

Jasmine Guillory is a *New York Times* bestselling author of novels
including *The Wedding Date,* the Reese's Book Club selection *The Pro-*
posal, and *Drunk on Love.* Her work has appeared in the *Wall Street*
Journal, Cosmopolitan, Bon Appétit, and *Time,* and she is a frequent
book contributor on the *Today* show. She lives in Oakland, California.

Mira Jacob is a novelist, memoirist, illustrator, and cultural critic. Her
graphic memoir *Good Talk: A Memoir in Conversations* was short-listed
for the National Book Critics Circle Award, nominated for three Eisner
Awards, long-listed for the PEN Open Book Award, named a *New York*
Times Notable Book, as well as a best book of the year by *Time, Esquire,*
Publisher's Weekly, and *Library Journal.* It's currently in development
as a television series. Her novel *The Sleepwalker's Guide to Dancing*
was a Barnes & Noble Discover Great New Writers pick, short-listed
for India's Tata First Literature Award, long-listed for the Brooklyn

Literary Eagles Prize, and named one of the best books of 2014 by *Kirkus Reviews*, the *Boston Globe*, Goodreads, Bustle, and The Millions. Her work has appeared in the *New York Times Book Review*, *Electric Literature*, *Tin House*, *Literary Hub*, *Guernica*, *Vogue*, and the *Telegraph*. She is an assistant professor in the Creative Writing Program at the New School, and a founding faculty member of the MFA Program at Randolph College. She is the cofounder of Pete's Reading Series in Brooklyn, where she spent thirteen years bringing literary fiction, nonfiction, and poetry to Williamsburg. She lives in Brooklyn with her husband, documentary filmmaker Jed Rothstein, and their son.

Leah Johnson is an eternal midwesterner and author of award-winning books for children and young adults. Her bestselling debut YA novel, *You Should See Me in a Crown*, was a Stonewall Honor Book, the inaugural Reese's Book Club YA pick, and named by *Time* as one of the 100 Best Young Adult Books of All Time. In 2022, Leah was selected for the NBC Out Pride 30 list, honoring "a new generation of LGBTQ leaders, creators, and newsmakers." Leah is a Lambda Literary Emerging Writers Fellow whose work has been published or is forthcoming in *Cosmopolitan*, *Teen Vogue*, and *Harper's Bazaar*, among others. The first installment of her debut middle-grade series, *Ellie Engle Saves Herself*, was sold in an eleven-house, seven-figure auction to Disney-Hyperion, and was published in May 2023.

Maris Kreizman is the host of *The Maris Review*, a weekly literary podcast. Her work has appeared in *New York* magazine, the *New York Times*, the *Wall Street Journal*, the *Atlantic*, *Vanity Fair*, *Esquire*, the *New Republic*, and more. Her essay collection, *I Want to Burn This Place Down*, is forthcoming from HarperCollins.

R. O. Kwon's nationally bestselling first novel, *The Incendiaries*, is being translated into seven languages and was named a best book of the year by over forty publications. *The Incendiaries* was a finalist for the National Book Critics Circle John Leonard Prize, and was a finalist or nominated for six other prizes. Kwon and Garth Greenwell coedited the bestselling *Kink*, which was a *New York Times* Notable Book and the recipient of the inaugural Joy Award. Kwon's writing has appeared in the *New York Times*, *Vanity Fair*, the *New Yorker*, and elsewhere. She has received fellowships and awards from the National Endowment for the Arts, Yaddo, and MacDowell. Born in Seoul, Kwon has lived most of her life in the United States.

Laila Lalami is the author of five books, including *The Moor's Account*, which won the American Book Award, the Arab-American Book Award, and the Hurston/Wright Legacy Award. It was on the long list for the Booker Prize and was a finalist for the Pulitzer Prize in Fiction. Her most recent novel, *The Other Americans*, was a national bestseller and a finalist for the Kirkus Prize and the National Book Award in Fiction. Her essays and criticism have appeared in the *Los Angeles Times*, the *Washington Post*, the *Nation*, *Harper's*, the *Guardian*, and the *New York Times*. She has been awarded fellowships from the British Council, the Fulbright Program, and the Guggenheim Foundation and is currently a distinguished professor of creative writing at the University of California at Riverside. She lives in Los Angeles.

Kiese Laymon is a Black southern writer from Jackson, Mississippi. Laymon is the Libby Shearn Moody Professor of English and Creative Writing at Rice University. Laymon is the author of *Long Division*, which won the 2022 NAACP Image Award for fiction, and the essay collection *How to Slowly Kill Yourself and Others in America*, named a notable book of 2021 by *New York Times* critics. Laymon's bestselling memoir *Heavy: An American Memoir*, won the Andrew Carnegie Medal for Excellence in Nonfiction, the Christopher Isherwood Prize for Autobiographical Prose, the Barnes & Noble Discovery Award, the

Austen Riggs Erikson Prize for Excellence in Mental Health Media, and was named one of the 50 Best Memoirs of the Past 50 Years by the *New York Times*. The audiobook, read by the author, was named the Audible 2018 Audiobook of the Year. Laymon is the recipient of a 2020–2021 Radcliffe Fellowship at Harvard. Laymon is at work on the books *Good God* and *City Summer, Country Summer* and a number of film and television projects. He is the founder of the Catherine Coleman Literary Arts and Justice Initiative, a program based out of the Margaret Walker Center at Jackson State University, aimed at helping young people in Jackson get more comfortable reading, writing, revising, and sharing on their own terms, in their own communities. Laymon was awarded a MacArthur Fellowship in 2022.

Min Jin Lee is the author of *Pachinko*, which was a finalist for the National Book Award for Fiction, a runner-up for the Dayton Literary Peace Prize, winner of the Medici Book Club Prize, and a *New York Times* 10 Best Books of 2017. A *New York Times* bestseller, *Pachinko* was also a Top 10 Book of the Year for the BBC, the Canadian Broadcasting Corporation, and the New York Public Library. *Pachinko* was a selection for Now Read This, the joint book club of PBS *NewsHour* and the *New York Times*. It was on over seventy-five best books of the year lists, including those of NPR, PBS, and CNN. *Pachinko* will be translated into more than thirty-five languages. President Barack Obama selected *Pachinko* for his recommended reading list, calling it "a powerful story about resilience and compassion." Lee's debut novel, *Free Food for Millionaires*, was a Top 10 Book of the Year for the *Times* of London, NPR's *Fresh Air*, *USA Today*, and a national bestseller. Lee is a recipient of fellowships in fiction from the Guggenheim Foundation (2018), the Radcliffe Institute of Advanced Study at Harvard (2018–2019), and the New York Foundation for the Arts (2000). In July 2022, she was inducted into the New York State Writers Hall of Fame. She is a writer-in-residence at Amherst College.

Will Leitch is a contributing editor at *New York* magazine, the founder of the late sports website Deadspin, and the author of six books, including the novels *The Time Has Come* (2023) and *How Lucky* (2021). He lives in Athens, Georgia, with his wife and two sons.

Ada Limón is the author of six books of poetry, including *The Carrying*, which won the National Book Critics Circle Award for Poetry. Limón is also the host of the critically acclaimed poetry podcast *The Slowdown*. Her new book of poetry, *The Hurting Kind*, is out now from Milkweed Editions. She is the twenty-fourth Poet Laureate of the United States.

Attica Locke's latest novel, *Heaven, My Home* (September 2019), is the sequel to Edgar Award–winning *Bluebird, Bluebird*. Her third novel, *Pleasantville*, was the winner of the Harper Lee Prize for Legal Fiction and was also long-listed for the Baileys Women's Prize for Fiction. *The Cutting Season* was the winner of the Ernest Gaines Award for Literary Excellence. Her first novel, *Black Water Rising*, was nominated for an Edgar Award, an NAACP Image Award, as well as an L.A. Times Book Prize, and was short-listed for the Women's Prize for Fiction. A former fellow at the Sundance Institute's Feature Filmmakers lab, Locke works as a screenwriter as well. Most recently, she was a writer and producer on Netflix's *When They See Us* and the upcoming Hulu adaptation of *Little Fires Everywhere*. A native of Houston, Texas, Attica lives in Los Angeles, California, with her husband and daughter.

Patricia Lockwood is the author of the novel *No One Is Talking About This*, a 2021 Booker Prize finalist and one of the *New York Times Book Review*'s 10 Best Books of 2021, and the memoir *Priestdaddy*, one of the *New York Times Book Review*'s 10 Best Books of 2017, as well as the poetry collections *Motherland Fatherland Homelandsexuals* and

Balloon Pop Outlaw Black. Her writing has appeared in the *New York Times*, the *New Yorker*, the *New Republic*, and the *London Review of Books*, where she is a contributing editor.

Carmen Maria Machado is the author of the bestselling memoir *In the Dream House* and the award-winning short story collection *Her Body and Other Parties*. Her essays, fiction, and criticism have appeared in the *New Yorker*, the *New York Times*, *Granta*, *Vogue*, *This American Life*, *The Believer*, *Guernica*, and elsewhere.

Rebecca Makkai's last novel, *The Great Believers*, was a finalist for both the Pulitzer Prize and the National Book Award; it was the winner of the Andrew Carnegie Medal for Excellence in Fiction, the Stonewall Book Award, the Clark Prize, and the L.A. Times Book Prize; and it was one of the *New York Times* 10 Best Books of 2018. Her other books are the novels *The Borrower* and *The Hundred-Year House*, and the collection *Music for Wartime*—four stories from which appeared in *The Best American Short Stories*. A 2022 Guggenheim Fellow, Rebecca is on the MFA faculties of the University of Nevada, Reno at Lake Tahoe and Northwestern University, and is artistic director of StoryStudio Chicago.

Megan Mayhew-Bergman is the author of three books with Scribner, the latest of which is *How Strange a Season*. She is at work on a biography of the International Sweethearts of Rhythm and currently teaches at Middlebury College, where she serves as the director of the Bread Loaf Environmental Writers' Conference.

Elizabeth McCracken is the author of four novels (*The Giant's House, Niagara Falls All Over Again, Bowlaway,* and *The Hero of This Book*); three collections of short stories (*Here's Your Hat What's Your Hurry, Thunderstruck & Other Stories,* and *The Souvenir Museum*), and a memoir (*An Exact Replica of a Figment of My Imagination*). Her stories have been anthologized in *The Best American Short Stories* and have won the O. Henry Prize and the Pushcart Prize.

Dantiel W. Moniz is the recipient of a National Book Foundation 5 Under 35 Award, a Pushcart Prize, a MacDowell Fellowship, and the Alice Hoffman Prize for Fiction. Her debut collection, *Milk Blood Heat*, is the winner of a Florida Book Award, and was a finalist for the PEN/Jean Stein Book Award, the PEN/Robert W. Bingham Prize, and the New York Public Library Young Lions Fiction Award, as well as long-listed for the Dylan Thomas Prize. Her writing has appeared in the *Paris Review*, *Harper's Bazaar*, *American Short Fiction*, *Tin House*, and elsewhere. Moniz is an assistant professor at the University of Wisconsin–Madison, where she teaches fiction.

Liz Moore is the author of four novels, most recently the *New York Times* bestselling *Long Bright River*. Her short fiction and creative nonfiction have been published in such venues as *Tin House* and the *New York Times*. Her novels have been translated into more than twenty languages. The winner of a 2014 Rome Prize in Literature, Moore lives in Philadelphia and teaches in the MFA program in Creative Writing at Temple University.

Amanda Mull is a staff writer at the *Atlantic*, where she covers health and consumerism and writes Material World, a column on consumer culture. She joined the publication in 2018, after a decade spent working in the fashion industry and writing for publications including *Rolling Stone*, *Elle*, *Vox*, *Glamour*, and *InStyle*. She's a native of Atlanta, Georgia, and a graduate of the University of Georgia.

Celeste Ng is the number one *New York Times* bestselling author of *Everything I Never Told You*, *Little Fires Everywhere*, and *Our Missing*

Hearts. Ng is the recipient of fellowships from the National Endowment for the Arts and the Guggenheim Foundation, and her work has been published in over thirty languages.

Sara Nović is the author of the *New York Times* bestselling novel *True Biz*, as well as the books *Girl at War* and *America Is Immigrants*. She has an MFA in fiction and literary translation from Columbia University, and is an instructor of creative writing and Deaf studies.

Alissa Nutting is a screenwriter and showrunner, most recently of *Made for Love* on HBO Max, based on her *New York Times* Editors' Choice novel of the same name, as well as the animated series *Teenage Euthanasia* on Adult Swim and HBO Max. She is also author of the novel *Tampa* and the collection *Unclean Jobs for Women and Girls* from Ecco Books.

Susan Orlean has been a staff writer at the *New Yorker* since 1992. She is the author of eleven books, including *The Library Book*, *The Orchid Thief*, and *On Animals*. She is the recipient of a Guggenheim Fellowship, a Nieman Fellowship, and the Marfield Prize. She lives in Los Angeles.

Lauren Oyler is a critic and novelist whose work appears regularly in the *New Yorker*, the *New York Times*, *Harper's*, the *London Review of Books*, and other publications. Her debut novel, *Fake Accounts*, was published in 2021.

Morgan Parker is a poet, essayist, and novelist. She is the author of the young adult novel *Who Put This Song On?* and the poetry collections *Other People's Comfort Keeps Me Up at Night*, *There Are More Beautiful Things Than Beyoncé*, and *Magical Negro*, which won the 2019 National Book Critics Circle Award for poetry. She is the recipient of a National Endowment for the Arts Literature Fellowship and a winner of the Pushcart Prize, and is a Cave Canem graduate fellow. She lives in Los Angeles.

Benjamin Percy is the author of seven novels—most recently *The Sky Vault* (William Morrow)—three story collections, and a book of essays. He writes Wolverine, X-Force, and Ghost Rider for Marvel Comics.

Deesha Philyaw's debut short story collection, *The Secret Lives of Church Ladies*, won the 2021 PEN/Faulkner Award for Fiction, the 2020/2021 Story Prize, and the 2020 L.A. Times Book Prize: The Art Seidenbaum Award for First Fiction and was a finalist for the 2020 National Book Award for Fiction. *The Secret Lives of Church Ladies* focuses on Black women, sex, and the Black church, and is being adapted for television by HBO Max with Tessa Thompson executive producing. Deesha is also a Kimbilio Fellow and the 2022–2023 John and Renée Grisham Writer-in-Residence at the University of Mississippi.

Maurice Carlos Ruffin is the author of *The Ones Who Don't Say They Love You*, a *New York Times* Editors' Choice that was also long-listed for the Story Prize, and *We Cast a Shadow*, which was a finalist for the PEN/Faulkner Award, the Dayton Literary Peace Prize, and the PEN Open Book Award.

Maggie Shipstead is the *New York Times* bestselling author of three novels and a short story collection. Her novel *Great Circle* was short-listed for the Booker Prize and the Women's Prize. She is a graduate of the Iowa Writers' Workshop, the recipient of a fellowship from the National Endowment for the Arts, and the winner of the Dylan Thomas Prize and the L.A. Times Book Prize for First Fiction. She lives in Los Angeles.

Mychal Denzel Smith is the author of the *New York Times* bestseller *Invisible Man, Got the Whole World Watching,* and *Stakes Is High*, winner of the 2020 Kirkus Prize for Nonfiction. He is a Puffin Foundation Fellow at Type Media Center, and Distinguished Writer-in-Residence at Hunter College. His work has appeared in the *New York Times*, the *Washington Post, Harper's, Artforum*, the *Oxford American*, the *New Republic*, the *Nation*, and more. In 2014 and 2016, TheRoot.com named him one of the 100 Most Influential African-Americans in their annual The Root 100 list. He was also a 2017 NAACP Image Award Nominee. Smith lives in Brooklyn.

Emma Straub is the *New York Times* bestselling author of six books for adults: the novels *This Time Tomorrow, All Adults Here, The Vacationers, Modern Lovers, Laura Lamont's Life in Pictures*, and the short story collection *Other People We Married*. She is also the author of three picture books, including *Very Good Hats*. Her books have been published in more than twenty languages. She and her husband own Books Are Magic, an independent bookstore with two locations in Brooklyn, New York.

J. Courtney Sullivan is the *New York Times* bestselling author of the novels *Commencement, Maine, The Engagements, Saints for All Occasions*, and *Friends and Strangers*. Her books have been translated into seventeen languages. Courtney's writing has also appeared in the *New York Times Book Review*, the *Chicago Tribune, New York* magazine, *Elle, Glamour, Allure, Real Simple*, and O, *The Oprah Magazine*, among many others. She is a coeditor, with Courtney Martin, of the essay anthology *Click: When We Knew We Were Feminists*. In 2017, she wrote the forewords to new editions of two of her favorite classic novels—*Anne of Green Gables* and *Little Women*. She lives outside Boston with her husband and two children.

Cynthia D'Aprix Sweeney is the author of the instant *New York Times* bestsellers *The Nest* and *Good Company*. She is a Barnes & Noble Discover Great New Writers' pick and her books have been named best of the year by *People*, the *Washington Post*, the *San Francisco Chronicle*, NPR, Amazon, *Real Simple*, and others. Her work has been translated into thirty languages. Sweeney lives in Los Angeles with her family.

Rachel Syme is a staff writer at the *New Yorker*. She has been living and writing in New York City for almost two decades, contributing to a smattering of publications including the *New York Times Magazine*, *Elle*, GQ, *New York* magazine, *Vogue*, the *New Republic*, and *Bookforum*. She is at work on a book about letter-writing with Clarkson Potter and an essay collection entitled *Magpie*, forthcoming from Knopf.

Hannah Tinti is the author of *Animal Crackers*, a runner-up for the PEN/Hemingway Award, *The Good Thief*, which won the Center for Fiction First Novel Prize and was a *New York Times* Notable Book of the Year, and *The Twelve Lives of Samuel Hawley*, which was a national bestseller and has been optioned for television. She is also cofounder and executive editor of the award-winning literary magazine *One Story*.

Bryan Washington is the author of *Family Meal*, *Memorial*, and *Lot*. He divides his time between Houston and Los Angeles.

Elissa Washuta is a member of the Cowlitz Indian Tribe and the author of *White Magic*, *Starvation Mode*, and *My Body Is a Book of Rules*. With Theresa Warburton, she coedited the anthology *Shapes of Native Nonfiction: Collected Essays by Contemporary Writers*. Elissa is an associate professor at the Ohio State University, where she teaches in the MFA Program in Creative Writing.

Michael H. Weber is an Oscar-nominated screenwriter and award-winning independent film producer. With Scott Neustadter, he adapted *The Disaster Artist*, which was nominated for Best Adapted Screenplay at the 90th Academy Awards. Their other writing credits include *(500) Days of Summer*, *The Fault in Our Stars*, *The Spectacular Now*, and *Our Souls at Night*. Weber graduated from the S. I. Newhouse School of Public Communications at Syracuse University in 2000. Born in New York City, he currently lives in Manhattan.

Meg Wolitzer is the *New York Times* bestselling author of *The Female Persuasion*, *The Interestings*, and *The Wife*, among other novels. A member of the MFA faculty at SUNY Stony Brook, Wolitzer cofounded and codirects BookEnds, a yearlong, noncredit program in writing novels. She was guest editor of *The Best American Short Stories 2017* and is host of the literary radio show and podcast *Selected Shorts*.

ACKNOWLEDGMENTS

Portions of this book appeared in *Poets & Writers* and the *Guardian*. I would like to thank:

The dedicated and vibrant #1000wordsofsummer community for inspiring me all year round. This book is for you and because of you.

All the authors who contributed their words to this project. You are talented, generous, and wise, and I'm lucky to know you.

Jacques Pierre Francois for sharing your immeasurable talents. Our collaboration means everything to me.

The patient and sharp-eyed Sarah Sturm for helping to shepherd this book through its growth.

My agent, Katherine Fausset, for your guidance, friendship, and vision for this book and my career as a writer. You're one of the best things to ever happen to me.

My editor, Ronnie Alvarado, for understanding what this book could be and helping me to articulate its true potential. I'm so lucky to have you on my side.

And these good people: Kristen Arnett, Priyanka Mattoo, Maris Kreizman, Jason Diamond, Isaac Fitzgerald, Emily Goldsher-Diamond, Josh Gondelman, Brooke Pickett, Laura van den Berg, Claire Cameron, Ladee Hubbard, Anne Gisleson, Alison Fensterstock, Caro Clark, Patricia Lockwood, Hannah Oliver Depp, Jason Kim, Katy Simpson Smith, Rien Fertel, Alex Chee, Catherine James, Megan Lynch, Chrissie Roux, Jasmine Guillory, Brad Benischek, Ajai Combelic, Morgan Parker, Megan Giddings, Lauren Groff, Mary HK Choi, Roxane Gay, Kayla Kumari Upadhyaya, Helen Atsma, and the kind folks at Petite Clouet Café, Pond Coffee, and Bar Pomona.

With love, as always, to my family.

CREDITS

"#1000wordsofsummer letter by Roxane Gay" © 2024 by Roxane Gay

"#1000wordsofsummer letter by Bryan Washington" © 2024 by Bryan Washington

"#1000wordsofsummer letter by Susan Orlean" © 2024 by Susan Orlean

"#1000wordsofsummer letter by Maris Kreizman" © 2024 by Maris Kreizman

"#1000wordsofsummer letter by Sara Nović" © 2024 by Sara Nović

"#1000wordsofsummer letter by Rumaan Alam" © 2024 by Rumaan Alam

"#1000wordsofsummer letter by Lauren Oyler" © 2024 by Lauren Oyler

"#1000wordsofsummer letter by Emma Straub" © 2024 by Emma Straub

"#1000wordsofsummer letter by Chris Gonzalez" © 2024 by Chris Gonzalez

"#1000wordsofsummer letter by Benjamin Percy" © 2024 by Benjamin Percy

"#1000wordsofsummer letter by Mira Jacob" © 2024 by Mira Jacob

"#1000wordsofsummer letter by Laura van den Berg" © 2024 by Laura van den Berg

"#1000wordsofsummer letter by Carmen Maria Machado" © 2024 by Carmen Maria Machado

"#1000wordsofsummer letter by Courtney Sullivan" © 2024 by Courtney Sullivan

"#1000wordsofsummer letter by Amanda Mull" © 2024 by Amanda Mull

"#1000wordsofsummer letter by Rebecca Carroll" © 2024 by Rebecca Carroll

"#1000wordsofsummer letter by Ada Limón" © 2024 by Ada Limón

"#1000wordsofsummer letter by R. O. Kwon" © 2024 by R. O. Kwon

"#1000wordsofsummer letter by Cynthia Sweeney" © 2024 by Cynthia Sweeney

"#1000wordsofsummer letter by Elissa Washuta" © 2024 by Elissa Washuta

"#1000wordsofsummer letter by Alexander Chee" © 2024 by Alexander Chee

"#1000wordsofsummer letter by Maggie Shipstead" © 2024 by Maggie Shipstead

"#1000wordsofsummer letter by Deesha Philyaw" © 2024 by Deesha Philyaw

"#1000wordsofsummer letter by Jasmine Guillory" © 2024 by Jasmine Guillory

"#1000wordsofsummer letter by Kristen N. Arnett" © 2024 by Kristen N. Arnett

"#1000wordsofsummer letter by Attica Locke" © 2024 by Attica Locke

"#1000wordsofsummer letter by Megan Abbott" © 2024 by Megan Abbott

"#1000wordsofsummer letter by Min Jin Lee" © 2024 by Min Jin Lee

"#1000wordsofsummer letter by Lauren Groff" © 2024 by Lauren Groff

"#1000wordsofsummer letter by Andrew Sean Greer" © 2024 by Andrew Sean Greer

"#1000wordsofsummer letter by Camille Dungy" © 2024 by Camille Dungy

"#1000wordsofsummer letter by Megan Giddings" © 2024 by Megan Giddings

"#1000wordsofsummer letter by Isaac Fitzgerald" © 2024 by Isaac Fitzgerald

"#1000wordsofsummer letter by Hannah Tinti" © 2024 by Hannah Tinti

"#1000wordsofsummer letter by Michael H. Weber" © 2024 by Michael H. Weber

"#1000wordsofsummer letter by Celeste Ng" © 2024 by Celeste Ng

"#1000wordsofsummer letter by Elizabeth McCracken" © 2024 by Elizabeth McCracken

"#1000wordsofsummer letter by Will Leitch" © 2024 by Will Leitch

"#1000wordsofsummer letter by Maurice Ruffin" © 2024 by Maurice Ruffin

"#1000wordsofsummer letter by Rachel Syme" © 2024 by Rachel Syme

"#1000wordsofsummer letter by Morgan Parker" © 2024 by Morgan Parker

"#1000wordsofsummer letter by Kiese Laymon" © 2024 by Kiese Laymon

"#1000wordsofsummer letter by Melissa Febos" © 2024 by Melissa Febos

"#1000wordsofsummer letter by Alissa Nutting" © 2024 by Alissa Nutting

"#1000wordsofsummer letter by Liz Moore" © 2024 by Liz Moore

"#1000wordsofsummer letter by Laila Lalami" © 2024 by Laila Lalami

"#1000wordsofsummer letter by Megan Mayhew Bergman" © 2024 by Megan Mayhew Bergman

"#1000wordsofsummer letter by Rebecca Makkai" © 2024 by Rebecca Makkai

"#1000wordsofsummer letter by Meg Wolitzer" © 2024 by Meg Wolitzer

"#1000wordsofsummer letter by Mychal Denzel Smith" © 2024 by Mychal Denzel Smith

"#1000wordsofsummer letter by Josh Gondelman" © 2024 by Josh Gondelman

"#1000wordsofsummer letter by Dantiel W. Moniz" © 2024 by Dantiel W. Moniz

"#1000wordsofsummer letter by Leah Johnson" © 2024 by Leah Johnson

"#1000wordsofsummer letter by Patricia Lockwood" © 2024 by Patricia Lockwood

ABOUT THE AUTHOR

Jami Attenberg is a *New York Times* bestselling author of seven books of fiction, including *The Middlesteins* and *All Grown Up*, and, most recently, a memoir, *I Came All This Way to Meet You: Writing Myself Home*. She has written for the *New York Times Magazine*, the *New Yorker*, the *Wall Street Journal*, the *Sunday Times* (UK), and the *Guardian*. She created the annual online group writing accountability project #1000wordsofsummer in 2018. Her work has been published in sixteen languages. She lives in New Orleans.